CLASSIC MUNSTER HURLING FINALS

CLASSIC MUNSTER HURLING FINALS

SEAMUS J. KING

GILL & MACMILLAN

Gill & Macmillan Ltd

Hume Avenue, Park West, Dublin 12

with associated companies throughout the world

www.gillmacmillan.ie

© Seamus J. King 2007

978 07171 3920 0

Index compiled by Cover to Cover

Design and print origination by O'K Graphic Design, Dublin

Printed by ColourBooks Ltd, Dublin

This book is typeset in 12/16 pt Giovanni Book.

The paper used in this book comes from the wood pulp of managed forests.
For every tree felled, at least one tree is planted, thereby renewing natural
resources.

A CIP catalogue record for this book is available from the British Library.

5 4 3 2 1

Contents

Preface

When I was asked to write a book on classic Munster finals, my first reaction was: What is a classic hurling match? I was informed that a 'classic' was a game that I believed to be above the ordinary, something exceptional, a contest that I considered to be somewhat memorable.

On such occasions it can be rewarding to consult a dictionary. I found that 'classic', an adjective, means something that is 'judged over a period of time to be of the highest quality and outstanding of its kind'. Under that criterion many of the games chosen by me as classic would not reach the standard. For instance, the 1978 final was a very poor game until the final ten or fifteen minutes.

So, one has to go back to one's own personal judgment, and I have to admit that the choice of finals in this book is very much a personal one, an arbitrary selection, which I shall attempt to justify.

Most of the games involved produced a result that was not quite expected, that went against the accepted wisdom of the time and created a level of euphoria or disappointment above the ordinary. As well, many of the games produced enormous efforts on the part of the players to achieve the desired result.

In 1952 Tipperary were confident of making it four in a row and Cork were equally determined to prevent it. It produced a game of high intensity.

It was somewhat different in 1955. Clare were the giant killers and Limerick were given little chance. On the day Clare performed below themselves, while Limerick excelled and produced a thrilling victory.

In 1960 Cork and Tipperary were striving for supremacy in Munster after a few years of stalemate, and the final produced a contest of passionate commitment on both sides before Tipperary shaded it.

There was a failure to recognise Waterford's challenge in 1963 although they had triumphed in the previous two encounters with Tipperary, the more recent in the league final. Tipperary were Munster and All-Ireland champions and there was a sense of shock when Waterford won 0-11 to 0-8.

The final in 1966 was different. Cork's victory marked their return after ten years in the doldrums, a much longer period of time than Cork were used to. The victory brought a huge sense of excitement and well-being to the county's supporters, so long starved of victory.

Tipperary's victory in 1971 came after losing to Limerick three times in the league earlier in the year. There was little between the sides and Limerick would have been fancied on the basis of the earlier encounters. Fortunes in the game swung to and fro during the hour until they finally sided with Tipperary.

The 1973 final was a repeat, with fortune this time swinging in Limerick's direction. Again, it was an intense struggle that came down to a puck of the ball in the end. It also had the *frisson* of controversy — was it a point? — to add to the excitement and make it a contest to be remembered.

Cork beat Clare in 1978, but there was a huge weight of expectation on Clare going into the final. The weight was even heavier at half-time as they appeared to have done enough in the first half to justify the expectation. And then, to the huge disappointment of the Clare following, it didn't quite turn out as expected.

The 1980 final is very special to Limerick. It was a long overdue triumph, wiping out the memories of a succession of major defeats by Cork. Cork were going for a record sixth victory and were fancied to win against a county they had more often defeated than lost to, but Limerick sprang a great surprise with a stunning victory.

Limerick made it a double when they defeated Clare in the 1981 decider. After a very exciting championship it came down to these two teams in a rare Munster final without either Cork or Tipperary. The verdict hung in the balance until Joe McKenna scored his third goal ten minutes from the end to tilt it Limerick's way.

In 1984 Tipperary were seeking to return from the hurling wilderness after thirteen years and appeared set to make the breakthrough with six minutes to go, when they led by four points. But in a stunning reversal of fortunes, Cork swiped the cup of success from their lips and left the Tipperary players and supporters alike gasping in disbelief.

What was agony in 1984 became ecstasy in 1987, when Tipperary finally ended the 'famine'. What made this final so memorable was that the victory didn't come until extra time in a replay, and when it came it was like a dam bursting, with some great goals and an overflowing of emotion from the Tipperary supporters.

Cork gave their response in 1990. Tipperary experienced few successes in Páirc Uí Chaoimh, but they travelled to this final as All-Ireland champions and were confident of improving their record at the venue. Cork had other ideas, plus a grievance of being likened to donkeys in an unfortunate aside by the Tipperary manager, and proved themselves thoroughbreds.

There was a lot of tit-for-tat between Cork and Tipperary during these years and the 1991 final was another episode in the rivalry between the sides. This final was again a replay and at half-time some Cork wags were regretting they hadn't gone to Killarney for the football decider, so far were they in front. But the game changed dramatically in the second half as a result of some stunning goals, and Tipperary triumphed.

It appeared that Clare were destined to win the 1994 final. They had overcome Tipperary earlier on and appeared to be on the way to a historic breakthrough. Limerick, however, had proved they were also contenders when they dismissed Cork, and the sides came together for the final. The pundits may have favoured Clare, but it was Limerick who were on top from the word go and recorded a convincing victory.

Clare eventually made it in 1995 when they overcame Limerick at Thurles. In a reversal of the previous year's result, Clare dominated this final. It was a wonderful day for the Banner and the euphoria expressed by their supporters as they flowed on to Semple Stadium after the final whistle was a joy to behold.

Clare came back in 1997 to consolidate their position as a hurling force. There was something unforgettable for Clare in this victory, their first over Tipperary in a Munster final. Tipperary would have fancied their chances and may have been slight favourites, but they had no answer to the power hurling and great eagerness of their opponents on the day.

Waterford had been a long time in the hurling doldrums before they made the breakthrough in 2002. Tipperary were the bookies' favourites for the final, but Waterford had other ideas. The game hung in the balance for three-quarters of an hour, but a goal by Waterford's Tony Browne opened the floodgates, and they were rampant during the final ten minutes.

Waterford repeated their success two years later in 2004 when they took Cork's scalp in the final. The fact that they hadn't beaten Cork in a final for forty-five years made them underdogs. The game hung in the balance until the end, but Waterford held on to triumph by a point.

One hundred and twelve teams contested the finals between 1950 and 2005. Cork led the way with 38 appearances, followed by Tipperary with 32, Limerick with 15, Clare with 14 and Waterford with 13.

On a statistical basis Cork should feature in the greater number of finals, but they appear in ten only, whereas Tipperary feature in eleven. The only excuse I can give for the balance in favour of the latter is my native Tipperary bias! Limerick are represented in seven finals, Clare in six and Waterford in four.

This is a personal selection based on my own experience and my attendance at finals over many years. It is by no means a definitive list of classic Munster finals during the period, and the games included are not necessarily the best finals during these years. However, they all contain some ingredients that make them particularly special and memorable in my estimation. Just as the finals themselves brought me a high level of excitement and entertainment, I hope that the accounts of them will bring some vicarious satisfaction to the reader.

1952: Cork deprive Tipperary of four in a row

The Munster final in 1952 added a new chapter to the intense rivalry between Cork and Tipperary. For three years Tipperary had been on top of the hurling world. Their only setback was a league defeat by Wexford the previous October. This was regarded as only a minor blip along the route to continued hurling dominance, and this opinion was confirmed by victories over Cork, Clare, Galway and Limerick to qualify for the league final against Wexford at Croke Park on 20 April.

In a preview to this game the *Tipperary Star* wrote about the champions 'who this year hope, not alone to complete the league and championship double, but to equal Cork's record of four All-Irelands in a row'. Tipperary did defeat Wexford, albeit by the minimum of margins, on a scoreline of 4-7 to 4-6 to make it three All-Irelands and three National Leagues in a row. It did take a Pat Stakelum point from a free in the last minute to secure victory after Nicky Rackard had scored two twenty-one yard frees in the last ten minutes.

TIPPERARY

Tony Reddin

Michael Maher	Tony Brennan	John Doyle
Séamus Bannon	Pat Stakelum (CAPT.)	Tommy Doyle

Phil Shanahan   John Hough

Eddie Ryan	Mick Ryan	Timmy Ryan
Jim Ryan	Sonny Maher	Philip Maher

This game was known as the 'home' final, and Tipperary played New York in the league final at Croke Park on 18 May, winning by 6-14 to 2-5. They had one more engagement before the Munster championship, against Galway at Mitchum Stadium, London, on 1 June. A depleted Tipperary side drew 2-4 to 1-7, but the report stated they should have won comfortably had they not concentrated on going for goals against a side that had the outstanding Seánie Duggan between the posts.

As well as being on top in the field of play, Tipperary were also making waves at administrative level in the GAA. The new President of the GAA, Vincent O'Donoghue, was from Lismore, but his mother was Josephine Mackey from near Moycarkey village. On assuming the presidency, O'Donoghue was replaced as Munster Council chairman by Gerry O'Keeffe of Clonmel. In the course of his last meeting as Munster chairman, held at Clonmel, there was controversy about the price of match programmes for the Cork-Limerick Munster championship semi-final game played at Thurles on 22 June. According to O'Donoghue, sixpence was 'a ridiculous price to charge for the official programme'. It was decided that in future the council would control the price of programmes, which were not to be more than three or four pence. In the course of the discussion Tipperary secretary Phil Purcell defended the charge, stating that the Christian Brothers were responsible for the programme, and pointing out that whatever profit was made was being used for the advancement of games in the schools.

The Munster championship commenced with a first-round clash between Waterford and Clare at Waterford on 1 June. The game ended in a draw, 3-4 each. Waterford won the replay at Thurles the following Sunday by 3-7 to 2-4. The winners were drawn to play Tipperary in the Munster semi-final at Limerick on 29 June.

On the other side of the draw Cork defeated Limerick by 6-6 to 2-4 in the semi-final at Thurles on 22 June. Cork hadn't won a Munster final since 1947 or an All-Ireland since the year before that. Tipperary had beaten them for three years, in a first-round replay in 1949 and in the Munster finals of 1950 and 51. If Tipperary were to succeed once again in 1952 and go on to win a fourth All-Ireland, they would equal Cork's proud record achieved from 1941 to 44 and surpass Cork in the roll of honour for senior All-Irelands.

Desperate measures were required. Most of the stars of the great Cork teams of the 1940s had gone into retirement and it wasn't too clear how their replacements would fare against the experienced veterans of Tipperary. Of course the team included a leaven of the old guard, players such as the O'Riordan brothers Ger and Mick, Paddy 'Hitler' Healy and the inimitable Christy Ring.

Cork had already shown promise and had impressed when beating Limerick 6-8 to 2-5 in the Thomond Shield final at Limerick on 8 June. Being short a few players they had to make changes beforehand, but so successful was the selection that there was not a single switch on the team for the entire game. Paddy Dwane made an auspicious debut at centre field.

Cork had little trouble in disposing of Limerick in the Munster semi-final by 6-6 to 2-4 at Thurles two weeks later. In a preview of the game in the *Cork Examiner*, the commentator had this to say: 'In all honesty it must be admitted at the outset that neither from the Shannon nor the Lee will come the best fifteens ever. For the past few years selectors in both counties have been searching and probing for the material to vanquish Tipperary. So far they have failed and whether the champions of the past three years will this season equal Cork's second "four-in-a-row" remains to be seen. It is admitted on every hand that only one team in Munster can stop them — Cork, and after next Sunday we will have a good idea how the Provincial final will wind up.'

Cork made two changes to the team that won the Thomond Shield two weeks previously. Omitted were T. Furlong and P. Healy in the forwards, and they were replaced by Matt Fouhy and Liam Dowling.

CORK

Mick Cashman

Ger O'Riordan	John Lyons	Vinny Twomey
Willie John Daly	Mossie O'Connor	Seanie O'Brien

Joe Twomey   Paddy Dwane

Matt Fouhy	Josie Hartnett	Christy Ring
Mossie O'Riordan	Liam Dowling	Paddy Barry (CAPT.)

The game lacked the fire that invariably characterised a clash between the counties. In fact it was one of the tamest meetings within living memory between the sides and was more like a tournament game than a Munster championship semi-final.

In a comment on the game in the *Cork Examiner* during the following week, Rambler went through the performance of the team and was happy with most of what he saw, although he did have reservations about the full forward line. On the other hand he was of the opinion that it was difficult to judge because Limerick were so mediocre. He would not be surprised if there were changes both in positions and personnel for the

Munster final. In the meantime 'my advice to players is to lead a good, regular life and remember that in 52 we may show them a clean pair of heels once again.'

The following Sunday, Tipperary played Waterford at Limerick. With two games under their belt Waterford were expected to put up a show but played much below par in the game. Their team included only two players, Mick Hayes and Jackie Goode, from the side that became Munster champions in 1948. The public mustn't have given them much chance: only 17,000 spectators paying £2,308 attended. Tipperary led by 5-5 to 0-4 at the interval and were in front by 8-10 to 3-8 at the final whistle. There was a great display by veteran Mickey Byrne. John Hough and Phil Shanahan were outstanding at midfield, and Paddy Kenny and Mick Ryan starred in the forwards.

TIPPERARY

Tony Reddin

| *Mickey Byrne* | *Tony Brennan* | *John Doyle* |
| *Jimmy Finn* | *Pat Stakelum* | *Tommy Doyle* |

Phil Shanahan   *John Hough*

| *Ned Ryan* | *Mick Ryan* | *Séamus Bannon* |
| *Paddy Kenny* | *Sonny Maher* | *Jim Ryan* |

The stage was set for the Munster final at Limerick on 13 July. The gates opened at 11.30 a.m. and the spectators took up their places on a first come, first served basis. Admission to the grounds was two shillings, and four shillings and sixpence direct to the sideline. Close to 43,000 spectators turned up, an increase of nearly a thousand on the previous year. An estimated 8,000 cars were parked on the streets of the city. The skies were overcast and a strong breeze blew towards the city. The teams paraded behind the St Patrick's Pipe Band, Tulla. Cork were led by their captain Paddy Barry, and Tipperary by Pat Stakelum. The ball was thrown in by Dr McCormick of Hexham-on-Newcastle, who was escorted on to the field by Canon E. Punch of Limerick and Vincent O'Donoghue, President of the Association.

Tipperary lined out with the same team that played against Waterford, with the exception of John Hough who cried off through illness the morning of the game. Séamus Bannon came out at centre field to partner Phil Shanahan, and Timmy Ryan came on at left wing forward in place of Bannon. Tipperary lost Tommy Doyle through injury in the first ten minutes, and Jimmy Finn was a sick man before he went on to the field.

Cork made some changes, as Rambler had predicted, from the Limerick game. The team mentors had a major problem when it came to selecting the goalkeeper. Mick Cashman of Blackrock and his understudy, Jim Cotton of St Finbarr's, were unavailable through illness. The third choice, Seánie Carroll of Sarsfields, was under suspension. Dave Creedon of Glen Rovers was enticed out of retirement, and it was to prove most fortunate as he was to win three All-Ireland medals before finally hanging up his boots. Tony O'Shaughnessy was introduced at left corner back, with Vin Twomey at centre back, to the exclusion of Mossie O'Connor. Paddy Dwane, who had promised well, was regarded as a bit slow on the faster ground and was replaced at centre field by Ger Murphy. Matt Fouhy was replaced at right wing forward by Mossie O'Riordan, with Paddy Healy taking up the latter's position in the corner.

In a tense, gripping struggle Tipperary confirmed their position as pre-match favourites when they led by 2-5 to 0-5 at the interval, having played with the aid of the breeze. The game had opened at a rattling pace and in the first minute a stinging drive by Mick Ryan was diverted for a 70, which Pat Stakelum pointed for Tipperary's opening score. Cork fought back, but when Christy Ring centred, the ball was intercepted by Stakelum and cleared. This started a movement which ended in a free for Tipperary, which Paddy Kenny pointed. Soon after, Mick Ryan snapped up a loose ball and sent over the bar from about thirty yards. At this stage Tommy Doyle had retired injured and was replaced by Bobby Mockler. As a result of another strong Tipperary attack, Cork conceded a 70 which Stakelum also pointed.

Cork opened their account with a point by Christy Ring in the eighteenth minute. Almost immediately Tipperary responded with a goal. Paddy Kenny, who had moved out to half-forward, hit a low shot from fifty yards that slipped between several players to the net.

Soon after, the same player added a point to give Tipperary the lead, 1-5 to 0-1.

Cork's second score came from Liam Dowling, who eluded Tony Brennan in the twenty-first minute. At this stage Cork made a few switches. Mossie O'Riordan moved into the right corner position, with Paddy Healy moving to the left and Paddy Barry taking over as right half-forward.

Tipperary suffered a setback in the twenty-seventh minute when they had a goal by Jim Ryan disallowed. He was deemed to be in the square. As well, Cork had now established control at midfield and were delivering a greater supply of ball to their forwards. Liam Dowling, doubling on a high pass from O'Riordan, scored Cork's third point. Paddy Barry had a fourth for the winners soon after.

There were tense passages at both ends before Séamus Bannon went through for Tipperary and beat the Cork goalkeeper from thirty yards. Cork retaliated when Ring made no mistake with a free to leave the half-time score 2-5 to 0-5 in favour of the Munster champions.

Tipperary had shown some fragility in the back line during the final ten minutes of the first half. Cork, sensing this, upped their game in the second half and were inspired by a great solo run by Ring soon after the resumption, which culminated in a brilliant save by Tony Reddin. They gradually whittled away at Tipperary's lead while at the same time not conceding anything to their opponents' forwards.

Reddin was forced to bring off another great save

from Ring before the same player opened the scoring with a point after five minutes. Murphy and Twomey were now lording it at centre field for Cork, and the latter added a long-range point, reducing Tipperary's lead to four points. The excitement was intense as Cork attacked again and again, only to be repulsed by great saves from Reddin and great defensive work by John Doyle.

Then came a wonderful moment for the Cork supporters in the fourteenth minute when, in a hectic goalmouth clash, Liam Dowling, who was having an outstanding game for the winners, went full length to turn a ball, which seemed to be going wide, into the corner of the net for a decisive goal. It was the turning point of the game. (There was controversy about this score, as there was about different incidents in clashes between Cork and Tipperary down the years. The referee, Jimmy Vaughan of Lismore, having blown the whistle and having indicated a free against Tipperary, was spoken to by a Cork player. He then changed his decision and allowed the goal to stand.)

The goal left only a point between the sides. Soon after, Ring scored the equaliser and he then gave Cork the lead for the first time. Two more Cork points followed, a Liam Dowling score from play and Seánie O'Brien from a free, and they led 1-11 to 2-5 with ten minutes to go. The lead might have been greater but for some brilliant saves by Tony Reddin.

During the final ten minutes Tipperary made tremendous efforts to get the goal that would level the game. Revealing that intrepid spirit with which they had fought so many gallant struggles during their long successful reign, they stormed into the attack, and every player on the Cork team moved back to defence to prevent them scoring. Two frees taken by Paddy Kenny from the right wing proved fruitless, and still Tipperary strove for the vital score. Phil Shanahan and Bobby Mockler retired and were replaced by John Hough and Gerry Doyle. Mick Ryan switched to the half-back line to mark Christy Ring.

Gerry Doyle sent over the bar from sixty yards to give Tipperary their only score in the half. A goal was needed for victory. Cork conceded a 70 which Stakelum dropped in the square. There were fierce clashes before Willie John Daly came clear with the ball to relieve the pressure. Stakelum came at the Cork backs once again, this time on a long solo run, but the Cork rearguard cleared their lines.

Tony O'Shaughnessy, who was making his championship debut that day, recalls one incident that might have changed the result. When a Tipperary sideline cut came in to him, he pushed it out in front of him, but as he did, Séamus Bannon came from nowhere, pulled on the ball and drove it inches wide.

Christy Ring, who had come back to help the defence, went down injured in a thrilling goalmouth clash. He resumed after an interval with his head heavily bandaged.

With only seconds left, Tipperary still fought manfully to save the game. The excitement was intense and the cheering continuous as Stakelum, from a 70, sent the ball into attack once again. Backs and forwards pulled hard, the umpire signalled a wide, and the long whistle blew on a final score of Cork 1-11, Tipperary 2-6. Cork's pride was restored and Tipperary were deprived of the elusive four in a row.

Wild scenes of enthusiasm followed as hundreds of excited Corkmen rushed the field and chaired off Christy Ring and several other members of the team. The Cork colours were to be seen everywhere as the players were cheered to the echo on a magnificent victory.

There was huge delight in the Cork camp. Tim Horgan, in his account of the game, captures some of the jubilation: 'We all simply went wild,' recalled Eamonn Young, who was watching the game. 'Christy Ring was carried shoulder-high through the crowd, blood streaming down his face, blood he never felt, for all he knew was that Tipperary were stopped. "For the Doc . . . for the Doc!" he shouted at me as he nearly tore my arm away. I got the meaning. My brother Jim, a doctor, was one of the nine four-in-a-row men along with Ringey. Their record — the record of the time — was still intact whatever about the All-Ireland of 52.'

The *Tipperary Star* headline read: 'Bang Went the Anticipated Four-in-a-Row.' They commented: 'Every man of the Cork team pulled his weight to make it a unit of great fire and energy, which in the end toppled the champions from their pedestal.' Tipperary's defeat was due to their failure to hit even a mediocre standard at midfield, the loss of Tommy Doyle after ten minutes, and the fact that Jimmy Finn was ill. 'A general malaise hit the players. Only Reddin, Doyle, Stakelum and

Byrne added to their reputations.'

Camán, the reputable commentator in the *Limerick Leader*, gave a different perspective. He stated that 'many would agree that over-confidence could not be excluded. Tipperary, with the stiff breeze behind them started at too slow a tempo and some of their erstwhile scoring stars lost a few early opportunities of raising flags of golden worth by attempting the fancy stuff against a side that had no place for frills in their repertoire.' He also blamed the mentors, believing that they panicked 'as Cork ate into the Premier county lead, and ten minutes from the end the bug had been transmitted to the players via frequent incursions of "advisers" with every stop in the play.'

Tony O'Shaughnessy also suggests that Tipperary may have been complacent. He adds that it was a day when everything seemed to go right for Cork, but it was the opposite for Tipperary. He recalls the game as a marvellous experience, even if he was scared arriving as a twenty-one-year old at the entrance beforehand, and the crowds milling around making it difficult to get into the ground.

Pat Stakelum doesn't have many happy memories of the game. He recalls a sideline cut he took near the end. It was a beauty, but Cork cleared it and Phil Purcell, one of the mentors, came in and said he should have allowed someone else to take it and gone into the square. He has reservations about the quality of the refereeing and believes that Tipperary were the victims. On one occasion Jim Ryan was deprived of a goal when the play was called back for a free. On another occasion

Cork got the advantage. He admits that the Cork backs were tough and took no prisoners. They didn't give the Tipperary forwards time to settle and completely dominated them in the second half, confining them to a point. In the context of the successes of the previous three years the result was a huge disappointment. 'When I look back on these days they weren't all Easter Sundays. There were Good Fridays as well, and this was one of them,' he concludes.

CORK

Dave Creedon
(GLEN ROVERS)

Ger O'Riordan	*John Lyons*	*Tony O'Shaughnessy*
(BLACKROCK)	(GLEN ROVERS)	(ST FINBARR'S)

Willie John Daly	*Vincy Twomey*	*Seánie O'Brien 0-1*
(GLEN ROVERS)	(CARRIGTWOHILL)	(GLEN ROVERS)

Joe Twomey   *Ger Murphy 0–1*
(GLEN ROVERS)   (MIDLETON)

Mossie O'Riordan	*Josie Hartnett*	*Christy Ring 0-5*
(BLACKROCK)	(GLEN ROVERS)	(GLEN ROVERS)

Paddy Healy	*Liam Dowling 1-3*	*Paddy Barry 0-1*
(BALLINCOLLIG)	(CASTLEMARTYR)	(SARSFIELDS, CAPT.)

Subs: Matt Fouhy (CARRIGTWOHILL), *Willie Griffin* (SHANBALLYMORE), *Liam Abernethy* (CASTLEMARTYR), *Jimmy Lynam* (GLEN ROVERS), *Mossy O'Connor* (SARSFIELDS), *Jimmy O'Grady* (ST FINBARR'S), *Mossy Finn* (ST FINBARR'S), *Tom Furlong* (BLACKROCK)

TIPPERARY

Tony Reddin
(Lorrha)

Mickey Byrne   Tony Brennan   John Doyle
(Thurles Sarsfields)(Clonoulty-Rossmore)   (Holycross-
Ballycahill)

Jimmy Finn   Pat Stakelum 0-2   Tommy Doyle
(Borrisoleigh)   (Holycross-Ballycahill,   (Thurles Sarsfields)
capt.)

Phil Shanahan   Séamus Bannon 1-0
(Young Irelands)   (Young Irelands)

Ned Ryan   Mick Ryan 0-1   Tim Ryan
(Borrisoleigh)   (Blackrock)   (Borrisoleigh)

Paddy Kenny 1-2   Sonny Maher   Jim Ryan
(Borrisoleigh)(Boherlahan-Dualla)(Holycross-Ballycahill)

Subs: Bobby Mockler (Thurles Sarsfields) for Tommy Doyle, Gerry Doyle (Holycross-Ballycahill) 0-1 for Mockler. Also Tim Ryan (Borrisoleigh), Johnny Walsh (Boherlahan-Dualla), Michael Maher (Holycross-Ballycahill), Philip Maher (Holycross-Ballycahill)

REFEREE

J. Vaughan (Lismore)

2

1955: Limerick shock Clare

Clare were odds-on to win the 1955 Munster final. They had defeated the All-Ireland champions, Cork, by a point in the first round of the Munster championship and dismissed National League champions, Tipperary, by a similar margin in the semi-final. Although Limerick had defeated a highly rated Waterford team in the other semi-final, they were a young team and weren't expected to halt a rampant Clare gallop. The result was very different. The Shannonsiders ran Clare off the field and overwhelmed them so much that they had ten points to spare at the final whistle. Whether through over-confidence or an inability to cope with the sweltering conditions on the day, Clare were unable to rise to the Limerick challenge. The majority of the Clare team played below themselves, but credit must be given to the speed of Limerick. Their wing forwards Liam Ryan and Ralph Prendergast split the Clare defence and created an opening for Dermot Kelly to go on a scoring spree to which Clare had no answer.

The fact that Limerick and Clare were meeting in the Munster final was a sensation. Tipperary and Cork had met in the final for the previous five years. Not since 1938 had both teams failed to appear in the final, and on only six occasions since the commencement of the Munster championship had there been a Munster final pairing without either Cork or Tipperary.

There had been some anticipation of Clare's arrival as a hurling force. The previous year was regarded as one of the county's greatest years, culminating in victory in the Oireachtas competition. According to a review of 1954 in the *Clare Champion*: 'Hurling took on a new lease of life, and now the county senior hurling team is rated one of the four best teams in the country.' The review continued: 'The Oireachtas victory brought the dogged attempts of the past three years to fruition in that code, and the victories preceding it were seen by the biggest followings ever supporting a Clare team. The Saffron and Blue made a name for itself and Clare supporters, cognisant of that, turned out in huge numbers and in a deserving manner.'

The new-found strength in Clare hurling was reflected in the number of players from the county selected on the Munster team in the Railway Cup competition. There were five involved: Donal O'Grady at centre back, Des Dillon at centre forward, Jimmy

Smyth at right wing forward, Jackie Greene at full forward, and Matt Nugent was a sub.

Clare representatives also played a prominent part in the game between the Combined Universities and the Rest of Ireland. Jackie Greene played full forward for the Universities against Dan McInerney, who played full back for the Rest. Des Dillon also played for the Universities, and Donal O'Grady was drafted in for the Rest when Jim English cried off.

The new selection committee for the year included Garrett Howard (Feakle), Dinny Hickey (Tulla), Michael 'Haulie' Donnellan (Clarecastle), Tommy Small (Ardnacrusha), a representative of the county champions, St Joseph's, and Paddy Canny (Dublin, formerly of Tulla), who was an adviser on the non-resident players and didn't have a vote.

The build-up to the first-round championship game against Cork on 5 June was intensive. In spite of the setbacks against Galway and Tipperary in the league, hopes were revived in the weeks beforehand. The win over Kilkenny in a tournament at Birr on 22 May injected a new confidence.

The team picked to play against Cork showed a number of changes to that beaten by Tipperary in the league. Mick Leahy and Johnny Purcell were back at right corner back and left wing back in place of Mick Guinnane and Tom Fahy. Jimmy Carney came on at right wing forward in place of Liam Murphy. Jackie Greene moved from full to right corner forward, while Donal Carroll and Pat Halpin were replaced by Bill Stritch at full forward and Gerry Ryan at left corner forward.

This was the team pitted against the vast experience of Cork, who were going for their fourth in a row. The sides met at Thurles on 5 June. Clare had a dream start with a goal in the first minute by Jackie Greene, and another by Des Dillon later in the half. They were in a strong position at half-time. However, Cork stormed back in the second half and had levelled the match by the eighteenth minute. Clare appeared to have lost their chance, but a great team effort kept them in the game, and a late Jimmy Smyth point proved the winner on a scoreline of 3-8 to 2-10.

CLARE

Mick Hayes

Mickie Leahy   *Dan McInerney*   *Haulie Donnellan*

Noel Deasy   *Donal O'Grady*   *Johnny Purcell*

Dermot Sheedy   *Jimmy Smyth 0-2*

Jimmy Carney 0-4   *Des Dillon 1-2*   *Matt Nugent* (CAPT.)

Jackie Greene 2-0   *Bill Stritch*   *Gerry Ryan*

Sub: Gerry Browne

Two weeks later Clare played Tipperary at the Gaelic Grounds, Limerick, in the Munster semi-final. The game was played in fine but overcast conditions before 38,000 spectators. For fifty minutes of the game Tipperary were well on top but hadn't scored accordingly, leading by only 0-5 to 0-2 at the interval, and the low scoring continued after the interval. When Jimmy Carney scored the only goal of the game in the fiftieth minute, first-timing the rebound of a Tony Reddin save from a Jackie Greene shot, Clare took the lead by a point for the first time in the game. They held on doggedly to the end, winning by the minimum margin, 1-6 to 0-8. Dan McInerney at full back and Donal O'Grady at centre back were the stars of the victorious side. Afterwards Tipperary objected to the legality of Jimmy Carney's participation, but the case didn't stand up and Clare clung to their victory and looked forward to the Munster final.

꧁꧂

While Clare were qualifying for the Munster final, Limerick remained rank outsiders for provincial honours even when they defeated Waterford in the semi-final. In fact at the annual convention of the county board back in January, it was felt that greater attention should be paid to the development of Gaelic games among the youth of the city and county because the standard of senior hurling in the county wasn't very high at the time. Forgotten, apparently, was the county's success in the 1954 All-Ireland junior championship, from which a number of players were to graduate to the senior ranks.

This pessimism about the senior team's chances was confirmed in the first outing in the league at Kilmallock early in February when they were well beaten by

Tipperary 5-6 to 1-2. In his comment on the result in the *Limerick Leader*, Camán stated that Limerick 'have the raw material from which champions are made but have a long road to travel for perfection'. He added that about ten of the players on show had potential, but to reach it meant 'hard work, constant training, keen attention to the finer points of the code and the vital assistance of old students of the game in order to knock off the rough corners and produce the polish and perfection that is the forerunner of success.'

There was better news for Limerick in their next outing against Clare at Ennis. On their previous visit there in the 1953 championship they had suffered their biggest championship defeat ever, losing to the home side by 10-8 to 1-1. On this occasion there was still defeat but a much more encouraging performance. Only six points separated the sides at the final whistle, and the margin would have been much less had Limerick had a free-taker of any note. Limerick supporters believed their defeat was due more to their poverty of scoring forwards than any superiority of the opposition.

Limerick didn't qualify for the play-off stage of the league. They watched Tipperary and Clare play each other in the semi-final at Limerick on 17 April, a game that Tipperary won easily against a side in which the stars failed to shine. A week later Limerick had a final trial in which most of the top players in the county were on view. The problem for the selectors was that the Probables, the team that everyone thought might be representing Limerick in the championship, were well and truly outclassed by the Possibles.

At any rate the championship stole up on the county and they faced Waterford in the Athletic Grounds, Cork, on 22 May. The sides had met the previous year at Thurles with victory going to the Decies men by 4-3 to 0-1. Limerick believed the score didn't give their performance due recognition and pointed out that after fifty minutes the game was still open even though Waterford led by 2-1 to 0-1. Whatever the opinion, the fact remained that the Limerick forwards were very poor.

Probably on the basis of that game and their performances in the league, neutral pundits gave Limerick little hope. Instead, Limerick confounded the predictions with an all-out display of speed and craft and won by 4-5 to 3-5. Playing with a confidence and determination long missing from the county, Limerick thoroughly deserved their one-goal victory.

The new rules were in operation for the game. Earlier in the year Congress had passed the 'no stoppage' rule which ensured continuity of play. It was going to make a big difference in the preparation of teams. Gone now were the days of 'lying down' to 'get the wind'. A dry summer and fast pitches would make life difficult for veterans. Two unbroken half-hours amounted to a major change for teams used to taking 'breaks'.

Added to this was the new rule about substitutions, under which only three were allowed in the course of the hour. Waterford suffered under this rule. Their full forward, Mick Healy, suffered what appeared to be a nasty injury early on. He was taken off and replaced by

Tom Cheasty. However, Healy recovered and resumed play with Cheasty coming off. Soon after, Joe Conlan was injured and having been examined it was decided to replace him. Cheasty was called in again. Waterford had therefore exhausted their quota of subs after only eighteen minutes of hurling and before they had a score on the board.

This victory over Waterford got little notice outside the county. Most focus was on the second semi-final between Clare and Tipperary, played at the Gaelic Grounds on 19 June, the winners of which were expected to win out in Munster. In the meantime Limerick had an important challenge game with Kilkenny at Nowlan Park. The lineout saw the inclusion of Paddy Creamer at centre back and the return of Dermot Kelly to the attack. Seán Leonard got the nomination for the full forward position. Significantly, the names of Liam and Séamus Ryan of Cappamore were listed in the subs.

LIMERICK

Paddy Cunneen

Donal Broderick	*Paddy Enright*	*Jim Keogh*
Eugene Noonan	*Paddy Creamer*	*Jack Quaid*

Mick McInerney   *Jim Quaid*

Tommy Casey	*Dermot Kelly*	*Vivian Cobbe*
Paddy O'Malley	*Seán Leonard*	*Jimmy Fitzgibbon*

The team gave an encouraging performance, had another outing against Galway, and were disappointed when Kilkenny failed to fulfil another fixture in the Gaelic Grounds which was to be the final preparation for the Munster final.

───⊗⊗⊗───

In a preview of the game a week ahead of the Munster final, which was played at Limerick on 10 July, Camán summed up his hopes thus: 'Upsets have been the keynote of this championship right from the opening, and we now expect the Limerick lads to complete the job by silencing all the prophets with a resounding success.'

The Limerick selection for the final went for youth in a big way. This was to suit the weather conditions prevailing. A good spell of weather had created a fast sod in the Gaelic Grounds and the day itself turned out to be a scorcher. One of Limerick's stalwarts, Dermot Kelly, was declared fit for the fray after an earlier scare, and he was to be flanked in the half-forward line by two speedy players, Liam Ryan and Ralph Prendergast, the country's 440 yards champion who had come to prominence on the Limerick CBS Harty Cup team and the Limerick minors. Goalkeeper Paddy Cunneen, corner back Jim Keogh and wing back Jack Quaid had graduated from the successful All-Ireland junior side of 1954. It was a formidable outfit well prepared by the great Mick Mackey himself, but not many outside of Limerick recognised the team's potential, and Clare were the warm favourites on the basis of their victories over All-Ireland champions, Cork, and National League champions, Tipperary.

A crowd of 23,125 came to the Gaelic Grounds to see the final. The size of the crowd was an indication of the way the supporters felt about Limerick's chances. The beautiful sunny weekend lured thousands to the seaside and they listened in disbelief when the result of the game was announced over the radio around 5 p.m. In fact the failure to broadcast the final drove Joseph P. Crowley, 9 New Terrace, Cappamore, to write to the *Limerick Leader* on 23 July, complaining that two football matches were preferred before it. According to him 'there were Gaels in parts of Clare and Limerick who could not afford to attend, and also old Gaels who would like to hear the match'. He concluded by saying: 'It is a terrible shame for those who are the fault of it.' Radio Éireann probably felt, like most people, that the match would be no contest.

The teams were paraded by St John's Brass and Reed Band and the ball was thrown in by Dr Leo D'Mello, native-born Bishop of Ajmer, India, who got a rousing reception. Among the attendance was Séamus MacFearon, President of the GAA, who travelled all the way from Belfast to witness his first Munster final. Also present was the Cork hurling star Christy Ring, who watched his first Munster final in many years, having played in thirteen of the previous fifteen.

The headline in the *Limerick Leader* the following day summed up the result of the final thus: 'Shock Team Clare Shocked by Youthful Limerick Team.' A youthful and fleet-footed Limerick side scored a facile 2-16 to 2-6 victory over a Clare side that failed to perform on the day. With the exception of Mick Hayes between the posts, Dan McInerney in front of him and Jimmy Smyth in the forwards, the Clare players left their form behind them in the earlier rounds against Cork and Tipperary.

In the sweltering heat the Clare team failed so dismally that few reputations were enhanced. Limerick trainer Mick Mackey exploited the speed and youth of his charges and dictated the trend of play from early on. Eighteen-year-old Ralph Prendergast darted here and there with such pace that he left his pursuers gasping. The Ryans and the Quaids, Dermot Kelly, Vivian Cobbe and Gerry Fitzgerald all had the speed to drag their opponents out of place and leave them at sixes and sevens. As well as speed, these players had plenty of skill and craft and hurled with the fluency of a well-geared machine.

Jimmy Smyth got the Clare supporters into full voice with a couple of early points, but Limerick were quickly into their paces and Dermot Kelly opened their account with a point from a free after six minutes. Two minutes later he equalised with as fine a shot as was ever hit at the venue. Mick Hayes brought off two great saves from Vivian Cobbe and Liam Ryan before Kelly sent over his third point and put Limerick into the lead, which they never afterwards surrendered.

Limerick continued to dominate and they got a succession of points without reply from Clare. Ralph Prendergast, Kelly once again and Séamus Ryan were the scorers. Five minutes from the interval Smyth pointed a Clare free. Two further Clare attacks were repulsed before Smyth scored his, and Clare's, fourth point. Cobbe was narrowly wide for a Limerick goal, but Clare counter-attacked and Limerick had to defend strongly in the closing minutes of the half. The interval score was 0-6 to 0-4 in favour of the home side.

Mick Hayes saved a rasper from Kelly shortly after the resumption and a fine clearance by Dan McInerney reached Des Dillon, who was, however, beaten for possession by Séamus Ryan. A moment later Matt Nugent, with a great effort, forced a 70 which was dropped in the goalmouth. Cunneen saved, passed to Broderick who cleared to Séamus Ryan, and the latter's clearance reached Jerry Fitzgerald well out on the wing. His shot was going a few inches wide, but Cobbe cut loose from his marker and hand-passed the ball to the net. That was seven minutes after the restart. The Limerick supporters went stark raving mad and they grasped that a surprise was on.

There was more of the same to come. A long delivery from Jim Quaid was pulled down by Hayes in the Clare goal and sent out for a 70. Séamus Ryan lobbed it into the square. A fast move by Prendergast gave Kelly possession, and as he shot to the net Prendergast raced behind it to make sure the goalkeeper was beaten.

Limerick were now running riot. Kelly scored a near-in free and when Smyth gave Clare their first point of the half, there was scarce a cheer. Two further points by Kelly came as the third quarter petered out, and Limerick led by 2-9 to 0-5, with many spectators making for the exits.

A fine effort by Cobbe was wide before Kelly scored another couple of points. At this stage there was a brief flare-up, which resulted in the sending-off of Gerry Fitzgerald (Limerick) and Haulie Donnellan.

With five minutes to go Clare recovered some honour with two goals within a minute from Jackie Greene. With Clare only six points behind and the possibility they might force a draw, Cobbe rallied Limerick with a point. Smyth replied with a point. A great effort by Noel Deasy was just wide, to which Liam Ryan replied with a point. Limerick were complete masters in the end and their supremacy was reflected in three points by Kelly, who hit them over as fast as the Clare defenders could puck out the ball. The final score was Limerick 2-16, Clare 2-6, with Dermot Kelly's personal tally a hugely impressive 1-12.

LIMERICK

Paddy Cunneen
(St Patrick's)

Donal Broderick	*Paddy Enright*	*Jim Keogh*
(Dromcollogher)	(Ahane)	(Ballybricken)

Eugene Noonan	*Séamus Ryan* 0-1	*Jack Quaid*
(Dromcollogher)	(Cappamore)	(Feohanagh)

Tommy Casey   *Jim Quaid*
(Ahane)   (Feohanagh)

Ralph Prendergast 0-1 *Dermot Kelly* 1-12   *Liam Ryan* 0-1
(Claughaun)   (Claughaun)   (Cappamore, capt.)

Gerry Fitzgerald	*Seán Leonard*	*Vivian Cobbe 1-1*
(RATHKEALE)	(AHANE)	(ST PATRICK'S)

Subs: Mick Fitzgibbon (TREATY SARSFIELDS), *Aidan Raleigh* (BRUFF), *Mick McInerney* (TREATY SARSFIELDS), *Paddy O'Malley* (CAPPAMORE), *Benny Fitzgibbon* (TREATY SARSFIELDS)

CLARE

Michael Hayes
(ST JOSEPH'S)

Mick Leahy	*Dan McInerney*	*Haulie Donnellan*
(RUAN)	(SCARRIFF)	(BROADFORD)

Matt Nugent	*Donal O'Grady*	*Tom Fahy*
(ST JOSEPH'S, CAPT.)	(FAUGHS)	(FAUGHS)

Dermot Sheedy *Noel Deasy*
(FEAKLE) (SIXMILEBRIDGE)

Jimmy Carney	*Jimmy Smyth 0-6*	*Des Dillon*
(DOONBEG)	(RUAN)	(UCD)

Gerry Ryan	*Jackie Greene 2-0*	*Johnny Purcell*
(MEELICK)	(NEWMARKET)	(ST JOSEPH'S)

Sub: Gerry Browne (ST JOSEPH'S). *Also Bernie Hoey* (CLOONEY), *Des Carroll* (SCARRIFF), *J. J. Bugler* (SCARRIFF), *Charlie Murphy* (TULLA), *Bill Stritch* (CLONLARA)

REFEREE
C. Conway (CORK)

One of the spectators described the Clare hurlers 'like racehorses trying to match pace in an unequal contest with speed cars'. Another said: 'Mick Mackey not only trained that team but wired them as well to take power and energy from every turbine in Ardnacrusha.'

The Clare team and supporters accepted their defeat in a very sportsmanlike manner. When the Limerick supporters swarmed on to the pitch, members of the Clare team were among those to join in the congratulations.

In the aftermath of the game there was more emphasis put on Clare's defeat than any analysis of the merits of Limerick's success. There were many theories touted for Clare's collapse, the most common that many of the players were seen indulging before the game. However, nothing was ever proven in this respect.

The most likely explanation was over-confidence. Clare were giant killers coming into the final and Limerick were minnows. Everyone was predicting an easy Clare victory and some of this had to rub off on the players. There was also the fact that Clare paid Limerick no respect, didn't know much about them and were still influenced by the trouncing they gave them in the 1953 championship game at Ennis.

Much of the blame was laid on Donal O'Grady and his total inability to control Dermot Kelly. However, there was an argument that the fault was not so much with the centre back but with the wings who were unable to cope with Limerick's Prendergast and Ryan. In O'Grady's attempt to shore up the wings the centre gave way.

Added to the above was the element of surprise that Limerick brought to the game. Fast and talented, they moved with speed, thrived in the sweltering conditions and adjusted to the no-stoppage rule with ease. They had been well prepared by Mick Mackey and they had his wisdom on the sideline. As well, everything went right for them on the day as if Lady Luck were smiling on them.

One side of the debate on the result is encapsulated in a quote attributed to Mick Leahy in Ollie Byrne's book, *Saffron & Blue 1906–2006*: 'Was the Clare approach lackadaisical? Were the players mentally prepared for a Munster final? Remember Limerick had been in the doldrums since the late forties. Were the Clare supporters mentally prepared for one? Looking at old photos of the Clare crowd before the throw-in resembled a Mardi Gras carnival rather than the tense atmosphere of a provincial final: . . . Give us the cup and let us out of here!'

The result remains one of the most sensational outcomes in the history of Munster finals. It put back hurling in Clare for decades, four of which were to pass before they made the breakthrough in 1995.

3

1960: Cork v Tipp — A war of attrition

When Tipperary were beaten by Wexford in the 1960 All-Ireland final, their first defeat at this stage of the senior hurling championship since going down to Limerick in 1922, many attributed the defeat to the gruelling contest the team had endured in the Munster final against Cork. The game had been rated the toughest ever Munster final as each side strove for supremacy. It was the first time that Tipperary had defeated Cork in a Munster final since 1951. The sides had met twice in semi-finals since Cork's three in a row in 1954, and the honours had been shared. The 1960 final was to decide who would be the new kings of Munster.

Tipperary had an easy route to the Munster final.

They strolled home 10-9 to 2-1 against Limerick in the first round at Cork. Only 16,000 people attended. Matt Hassett of Toomevara, who had come to the attention of the selectors, had taken over from the legendary Mickey Byrne at right corner back and had a good game. Full back Michael Maher revealed he wasn't as fast as he once was. Kieran Carey was hampered by a recent appendix operation. Tom Ryan of Killenaule was in his element at centre field. Terry Moloney was eager, fit and able in goal.

Tipperary had one other change to the team that had won the National League final against Cork on 1 May. Donal O'Brien (Kickhams) was drafted in as sub goalie in place of Roger Mounsey (Toomevara). Tipperary had surprised even their own supporters with a fine display to take their ninth league title. At half-time their prospects weren't bright as they trailed Cork 2-5 to 1-5, and many of the team, particularly the forwards, were playing indifferently. The players were spurred to greater endeavour by the interval pep talk because they came out a changed side in the second half. They dominated the period so much that with a few minutes to go they led by 2-15 to 2-8. Then Christy Ring got a rather easy goal and this sparked off a Cork flurry, but no scores resulted and the final whistle saw Tipperary ahead, 2-15 to 3-8.

TIPPERARY

Terry Moloney

Mickey Byrne   *Michael Maher*   *Kieran Carey*

Mick Burns   Tony Wall   John Doyle

Theo English   Tom Ryan

Jimmy Doyle   Liam Devaney   Donie Nealon

Liam Connolly   Billy Moloughney   Tom Moloughney

Tipperary kept faith with the same side for the championship with the exception of Mickey Byrne, who retired from a long career after the league victory. They were in no way flattered by their comprehensive defeat of Limerick, who were unbelievably poor and disjointed on the day. The test against Waterford in the semi-final would be a much sterner one. Waterford were All-Ireland champions, having taken their second title against arch rivals Kilkenny the previous year. They had a match-winning centre field pair in Séamus Power and Phil Grimes. They had also impressed in putting away Galway by 9-8 to 4-8 in their first-round game.

The game was played at Limerick on 17 July and a crowd of 35,000 turned up. A great game was expected, but it turned out to be a flop. Although Waterford were missing John Kiely and Jack Condon on the day, their absence could not account for the inept performance of the team. The same team that had overwhelmed Tipperary by 9-3 to 3-4 in the previous year's championship were themselves overwhelmed by 6-9 to 2-7 on this occasion. Waterford flopped in a manner that was unbelievable. After the first quarter the game was no contest. A drenching shower of rain at the start of the game may have knocked some of the zip out of Waterford. Tipperary led 4-6 to 1-4 at the interval. For Tipperary there were great performances from the two Doyles, John and Jimmy. They were yards ahead of the Waterford players. Tony Wall, who couldn't manage Tom Cheasty the previous year, came out on top in this contest. The feeling in the county after the game was that Tipperary should beat Cork in the Munster final.

Cork had a bye to the Munster semi-final in which they played Clare at Thurles on 12 June. The team was going through a transition period and hadn't won a Munster final since 1956. A number of new players, Denis O'Riordan, Denis Murphy, Jerry O'Sullivan and Patsy Harte, had been introduced for the league campaign. The team performed better than expected and got to the final against Tipperary at the Cork Athletic Grounds. It was the veteran Christy Ring, with a personal tally of 3-4, who was their best performer on the day. Although the team went down there was hope for the championship.

CORK

Mick Cashman

Jimmy Brohan   *Denis O'Riordan*   *Seán French*

Denis Murphy   *Jerry O'Sullivan*   *Mick McCarthy*

Noel Gallagher   *Eamonn Goulding*

Patsy Harte	Terry Kelly	Pat Fitzgerald
Paddy Barry	Liam Dowling	Christy Ring

Cork were unimpressive against Clare and might have been surprised, winning by 2-12 to 1-11. A very underrated Clare side with the aid of a stiff breeze raced into a six-point lead after twenty-four minutes. Cork were lucky to get a goal just before half-time which reduced their deficit at the interval to five points. It did not reflect Clare's supremacy in the opening half. With the aid of the wind in the second half, Cork soon made the running and had gone ahead by 2-7 to 0-10 before the third quarter had elapsed. Cork supporters looked forward to a convincing victory. But Clare came back with a goal, and in the remaining minutes it might have been either side's game, with Cork coming through in the end by four points. Even if allowances were made for the wind, the wet sod and the burden of favouritism, it was still an unimpressive performance by Cork. Fewer than half their players performed with any conviction, and of the remainder some were at best mediocre and the rest could be written off. The prospects of beating Tipperary in the Munster final looked slim in the aftermath of the game.

CORK
Mick Cashman

Jimmy Brohan	John Lyons	Seán French
John O'Connor	Denis O'Riordan	Jerry O'Sullivan

Eamonn Goulding		Phil Duggan
Terry Kelly	Jim Young	Christy Ring
Pat Healy	Mick Quane	Paddy Barry

The Munster final was played at Thurles on 31 July. Tipperary made one change from their semi-final side. Billy Moloughney was dropped from the full forward line and replaced by Seán McLoughlin (Thurles Sarsfields). He went to corner forward with Tom Moloughney going into the full forward position. Another Thurles Sarsfields player, Ray Reidy, was drafted into the subs. The other subs were Donal O'Brien, Noel Murphy, Donal Ryan (Moycarkey-Borris) and Jimmy Finn. According to the *Tipperary Star* commentator, Winter Green, there were three solid reasons why Tipperary should win: Jimmy Doyle, Liam Devaney and Donie Nealon.

Cork made a number of changes to the side which defeated Clare. Mick McCarthy came in at wing back in place of John O'Connor and Jerry O'Sullivan went to centre back, exchanging positions with Denis O'Riordan. Terry Kelly moved out to centre field to partner Phil Duggan, with Eamonn Goulding going to centre forward. Joe Twomey and Liam Dowling replaced Jim Young and Pat Healy in the forwards.

A record attendance for Thurles of just under 50,000 spectators turned up for the final. A thunder shower during the preceding minor game drenched the crowd who, however, stuck it out to the end, forgetting about their sodden clothes in the thrills of the game. It was the first time in thirty-four years that Thurles had failed to produce a dry day for a major hurling game. A two minutes silence was observed, after the teams had paraded round the pitch behind the Moycarkey Seán Treacy's Pipe Band, in memory of William O'Dwyer of Donaskeigh who was for thirty years treasurer of the West Tipp GAA Board. The ball was thrown in by the new patron of the GAA and Archbishop of Cashel and Emly, Dr Tom Morris.

For the first half Cork had all the better of the play, with the Tipperary midfield failing inexplicably and the much-vaunted half-forward line being held firmly. With few opportunities Tipperary nevertheless had a goal lead at half-time. It was only in the third quarter that the home side at last started rolling. Cork's pace slackened and Tipperary got sufficient headway to keep them clear at the final whistle, despite a last-minute surprise goal from Cork.

For the Tipperary supporters, who had seen their team decisively defeat Cork in the league final a couple of months previously and sail through the All-Ireland champions, Waterford, in the semi-final, the first half-hour was something of a painful shock. Cork were yards faster to the ball. They simply tore through the Tipperary defence, obliterated their midfield, and yet the extraordinary thing was that despite all that superiority and ground advantage they were still a goal behind at half-time.

The main reason was the performance of the

Tipperary inside forward line, not the half-line on which so much was expected. Liam Connolly, Tom Moloughney and Seán McLoughlin rose to the occasion magnificently. Given half a chance they were able to add something to the scoreboard with the few opportunites that came their way.

The other contributory factor was Cork's failure to take their chances during their period of dominance. On the run of play they should have had more scores during the first half. They threw themselves into the game with abandon and gave an outstanding exhibition of first-time pulling on the ground and in the air, as if they were going to run Tipperary off the field. Perhaps the very speed of their exchanges prevented them from making the best use of their possession. They had nine wides to Tipperary's four during the opening half. It could be said that an odd streak of luck saved the day for Tipperary. On one occasion Ring hit the upright just at the bar: six inches more goalwards and the shot would have been in.

Tipperary followers were given little to cheer about in the opening half. There was no dominating play from the Jimmy Doyle-Devaney-Nealon half-forward line. Theo English and Tom Ryan (who went down injured three times during the game) were tied down completely by their opposites, Phil Duggan and Terry Kelly. For most of the first half the Cork pair completely outplayed the opposition and Kelly in particular was much too good for Tom Ryan. But their stamina-sapping display in the first half had consequences after the interval when Kelly faded completely and

Duggan was replaced.

In the opening quarter Cork were yards in front of what was generally regarded as a fast Tipperary team. Barry's goal in the first minute caught the backs napping. He was through the gap in a flash and gave the Tipp goalkeeper, Moloney, no chance. After McLoughlin's goal was disallowed, Jimmy Doyle had Tipperary's opening score, a point. Kelly and Quane pointed for Cork and Devaney for Tipperary to put three points between the sides. Then after Ring was inches wide, Moloughney pointed for Tipperary, followed by a goal by Liam Connolly to put Tipperary in the lead for the first time. Ring equalled with a point from a twenty-one yard free to leave the sides at 1-3 each. McLoughlin had another goal, but it was very quickly negated by another from Paddy Barry, which was followed by a second point from Ring.

Then came the best score of the game when Jimmy Doyle, from about forty yards out, sent in a low whistler which beat Cashman completely. The same player followed up with a point, and when the half-time whistle sounded, Tipperary were the most unlikely leaders by 3-4 to 2-4.

On the resumption it was Cork who were to the fore. Within a few minutes they had drawn level with three unanswered points, and Quane put them in front with a fourth. Moloughney then hit the net and the Tipperary jubilation was unbounded. Tipperary had another point to put three between the sides. Then Jimmy Doyle showed some of his old sparkle, scoring three unanswered points to put Tipperary six points clear.

A goal from Dowling cut Cork's deficit back to three, but Jimmy Doyle pointed once again. Points were exchanged and with time running out Tipperary were five points in front. Then came a goal by Quane, which lifted Cork's hopes of a dramatic ending. But Tipperary held out to the relief of their supporters with the final score 4-13 to 4-11 in their favour.

TIPPERARY

Terry Moloney
(Arravale Rovers)

Matt Hassett	*Michael Maher*	*Kieran Carey*
(Toomevara)	(Holycross-Ballycahill)	(Roscrea)

Mick Burns	*Tony Wall 0-1*	*John Doyle*
(Nenagh)	(Thurles Sarsfields, capt.)	(Holycross-Ballycahill)

Theo English   *Tom Ryan*
(Marlfield)   (Killenaule)

Jimmy Doyle 1-8	*Liam Devaney 0-1*	*Donie Nealon 0-1*
(Thurles Sarsfields)	(Borrisoleigh)	(Youghalarra)

Liam Connolly 0-1	*Tom Moloughney 1-1*	*Seán McLoughlin*
(Fethard)	(Kilruane-MacDonaghs)	(Thurles Sarsfields)

Subs: Jimmy Finn (Borrisoleigh), *Donal Ryan* (Moycarkey-Borris), *Noel Murphy* (Thurles Sarsfields), *Donal O'Brien* (Kickhams), *Billy Moloughney* (Kildangan), *Ray Reidy* (Thurles Sarsfields)

CORK

Mick Cashman
(BLACKROCK)

Jimmy Brohan	*John Lyons*	*Seán French*
(BLACKROCK)	(GLEN ROVERS, CAPT.)	(GLEN ROVERS)

Mick McCarthy	*Jerry O'Sullivan*	*Denis O'Riordan*
(GLEN ROVERS)	(GLEN ROVERS)	(GLEN ROVERS)

Phil Duggan 0-1   *Terry Kelly 0-1*
(GRENAGH)   (TRACTON)

Paddy Barry 2-0	*Eamonn Goulding*	*Joe Twomey 0-1*
(SARSFIELDS)	(GLEN ROVERS)	(GLEN ROVERS)

Liam Dowling 1-0	*Mick Quane 1-2*	*Christy Ring 0-6*
(SARSFIELDS)	(GLEN ROVERS)	(GLEN ROVERS)

Subs: John Bennett (BLACKROCK) *for Duggan, Denis Murphy* (GRENAGH) *for French, Noel Gallagher* (YOUGHAL) *for Twomey. Also John O'Connor* (CARRIGTWOHILL), *Seán O'Brien* (GLEN ROVERS)

REFEREE

Gerry Fitzgerald
(LIMERICK)

In the aftermath of the game commentators were divided in their opinions. For some it was the greatest Munster final ever; for others it was a tough, dour encounter in which players went beyond the rules of the game.

The reporter in the *Tipperary Star* was very definite in his opinion: 'Sunday's game has been hailed as the greatest Munster final ever played. It was not that by any means. It was fast and tough but there have been other more soul-stirring, body-tingling encounters than this one.'

In contrast, the commentator Winter Green in the same paper had no doubt it was the best final ever: 'Deep in the hearts of 50,000 spectators will be enshrined memories of a stupendous encounter, where manhood in all its glorious virility was the order of the day, where the extreme niceties of the game had to be laid aside, where for sixty minutes thirty men swung camans with a glorious abandon that was at times terrifying to the spectators, and where not a man of the thirty sustained severe injury during the hectic hour, and when it was all over there was almost complete unanimity among friend and foe alike that this was the greatest Munster final ever played.'

For the reporter in the *Cork Examiner* 'the raw elemental rivalry of our two greatest hurling counties was laid bare . . . and was almost frightening in its intensity. It drove players beyond the bounds of normal endurance; it fired them with a spirit, an unrelenting fury of sustained effort, which was most times heroic but sometimes ignoble. It was a struggle of hurling giants in which all things that constitute hurling parity, excitement and dedication to victory were magnified. It was a Munster final which, in the future, will still loom large, controversial, but quite unforgettable. It will be spoken of by some as an hour when uncontrolled tempers burst the bounds of good sportsmanship, but they will be in the minority. It will be remembered by the many as an almost unprecedented feat of hurling skill in stress, of fitness and fortitude. It will be recalled as the moment of truth and justification for a much-maligned Cork team who, almost to a man, wore the red jersey with distinction.'

In the light of such superlatives, what had the referee's report to say of the game? Limerick referee Ger Fitzgerald is no longer with us to give an opinion. Whatever report he filed for the Munster Council hasn't been retained. In one report of the game it is stated: 'The referee was probably right in erring on the side of leniency.' Paddy Barry and John Doyle were involved in fisticuffs on a number of occasions, and there were a few other incidents as well. In fact it was the sheer intensity of the exchanges in most cases, rather than anything untoward, that seemed to mark the game. The one untoward incident happened after the final whistle when some over-the-top Tipperary supporters attempted to engage Christy Ring in a fracas.

Tipperary full back on the day, Michael Maher, remembers the game as a good hard one, with no pulling of punches. The hurling was good and the determination fierce. He believes Cork were really up for it and they wanted a win for some of their veteran hurlers before they called it a day. Tipperary were equally determined to win. He reckons it was an intense game but not dirty, not a game 'you'd be ashamed to have played in'.

Terry Kelly, who had an outstanding game at centre field for Cork, recalls the incident where Jerry Doyle, in his tennis shoes, came on to the field and made some remark to Ring. It must have annoyed the Cork player because he took off after Doyle. While he was out of position a ball came in and his marker, Matt Hassett, was able to clear without any difficulty. He believes that Cork were really up for the game. Glen Rovers had the selection and they were determined to succeed, especially after their defeat in the league. They packed the team with Glen players, picked for particular positions, where they were believed capable of being most effective on their opponents. For instance, Paddy Barry was picked to be on John Doyle and Liam Dowling to mark Kieran Carey. Dowling normally played at full forward. Kelly knew long before the game that he would be marking Tom Ryan. He accepted that it was a very tough game and believes the reason was because Tipperary responded on the day with equal determination. He recalls John D. Hickey's match report calling the game one of the toughest he had witnessed.

Theo English remembers the game as the toughest he ever encountered against Cork, but not dangerously so. There were a lot of heavy shoulder tackles and a lot of digging in the ribs. He recalls John Doyle and Paddy Barry throwing down the hurleys and going at one another with their fists. He also recalls Larry Dunne, an undertaker from Clonmel, rushing to where Ring was involved in a fracas after the game. He put his head in at the wrong time and got a belt of a hurley from Ring. He got an awful slagging for weeks afterwards in Clonmel, but he came to be proud of the incident as it became a badge of honour to have got a belt from Ring!

4

1963: Waterford surprise Tipperary

Writing in the *Tipperary Star* in the middle of June 1963 about the prospects of different counties in the Munster championship, Gaelic games commentator Culbaire had this to say about his native county: 'Of all the top-grade counties Tipperary show least variation from day to day, a quality that may serve them well this important year.'

The year was important because the county was going for three-in-row All-Irelands, and it might have been four but for the defeat by Wexford in the 1960 final. Culbaire was expressing the general confidence within the county in Tipperary's prospects.

At this stage two first-round games had been played in the Munster championship. Limerick had defeated

Galway 3-9 to 2-7 at Ennis, and Cork had overcome Clare 4-15 to 2-11 at Thurles. The semi-final draws pitted Tipperary against Cork at Limerick on 30 June, and Waterford against Limerick at Cork Athletic Grounds a week later.

The general expectation was that Tipperary would qualify for the final. Cork hadn't been good for some time. As one commentator put it, they were 'shuffling and reshuffling the same hand for quite a few seasons with only intermittent gleams of success, such as reaching the league final against Kilkenny a year ago'.

The same expectation of an epic clash between the two rivals was absent in the build-up to the game. In place of the uncomfortable crowded embankments of two years previously, there was plenty of space for everyone who turned up at Limerick on 30 June, and much more besides. People were not expecting an epic.

Those that did turn up were set for a resounding Tipperary triumph; in the circumstances the supporters of the blue and gold had to settle for a win which lacked the clear-cut character one would have expected in the circumstances. The reason for the unconvincing result from a Tipperary point of view had less to do with the strength of the Cork performance and more to do with the weakness of Tipperary's effort. For one thing Tipperary were slow about settling down and Cork were a goal and a point up before Tipperary opened their account. Part of the reason was the slowness of the Tipperary half-back line of Burns, Wall and Murphy to get into the game. By half-time Tipperary had recovered somewhat to lead 2-3 to 1-4.

Tipperary had the breeze in the second half. They also made a number of changes, with Liam Devaney going full forward, Larry Kiely centre forward and Donie Nealon centre field to mark Terry Kelly. These changes had an impact and Tipperary edged in front by seven points, which included a superb point by Theo English from a sideline cut and an opportunist goal by Seán McLoughlin.

But Cork were unwilling to concede and a brilliant run of six points, with a Jimmy Doyle one sandwiched between them, reduced the margin to a dangerous two points. Tipperary steadied with a Nealon point and a second McLoughlin goal widened the margin again to six points. Harte reduced the margin by a point and the final score was 4-7 to 1-11 in favour of Tipperary.

TIPPERARY

Roger Mounsey

John Doyle   *Michael Maher*   *Kieran Carey*

Mick Burns   *Tony Wall*   *Michael Murphy*

Theo English   *Liam Devaney*

Jimmy Doyle   *Donie Nealon*   *Tom Ryan*

Mackey McKenna   *Larry Kiely*   *Seán McLoughlin* (CAPT.)

Sub: Liam Connolly for Kiely

A week later the second semi-final took place. Waterford played Limerick in the Athletic Grounds and came away with a reasonably comfortable victory, winning by seventeen scores to nine on a scoreline of 2-15 to 3-6. Waterford went into the game as favourites on the basis of their success against Tipperary in the league final. However, it was Limerick who made the early running. They played with speed, dash and fury for a long time with the inspiration of two early goals to spur them. These goals were focused on by the Tipperary followers, seeing in them a lack of certainty by the Waterford goalkeeper Ned Power on the ground ball. But Waterford never lost their poise and coolness, gradually established themselves and were level by the break.

Limerick went ahead by a point early in the second half, but gradually their effort began to fade and after Waterford got a rather fortuitous goal, they gradually assumed command of the game. A late Limerick goal could not affect the issue and Waterford deserved their six-point victory, which was achieved without the services of Tom Cheasty and with a less than fully fit Larry Guinan.

Deiseach had an interesting spin on the victory in the following week's *Waterford News and Star*. After suggesting that Limerick hoped as a result of a rampant start to hammer Waterford into early subjection, he went on to state: 'Their pre-match plan was based on the long-exploded fallacy: "Lead Waterford and you win." Limerick lived in a fool's paradise. Before the Munster senior hurling semi-final had run its course, Limerick had been taught a hard lesson and Waterford, hurling well within themselves, their experience, coolness under pressure and fighting spirit always in evidence, crashed through to the Munster final and another battle with Tipperary.'

WATERFORD

Ned Power

Tom Cunningham   *Austin Flynn*   *John Byrne*

Larry Guinan   *Martin Óg Morrissey*   *Jim Irish*

Joe Condon (CAPT.)   *Martin Dempsey*

Michael Flannelly   *Jim Barron*   *Frankie Walsh*

Séamus Power   *Charlie Ware*   *Phil Grimes*

Subs: John Meaney for Morrissey, Sonny Walsh for Flynn

The stage was set for a Tipperary-Waterford clash in the Munster final at Cork on 28 July. While deep down Tipperary followers would not concede favouritism to Waterford, in fact they deserved that tag on the basis of two victories in the previous two meetings between the sides. Waterford had come out on top in the Oireachtas and the league, regardless of their twenty-point drubbing by Tipperary in the previous year's Munster final. This victory dominated Tipperary's thinking in the approach to the game, even though Waterford lacked Frankie Walsh and Tom Cheasty on this occasion.

Even Waterford's victory in the league final at Croke Park on 5 May was regarded within the county as a blip rather than a reflection of Tipperary's inferiority. In fact Waterford deserved a bigger margin of victory than the 2-15 to 4-7 outcome. Fitter and faster, Waterford played sparkling hurling, particularly in the second half, and came back several times to equalise and eventually win. In fact Waterford revealed a lot of strengths. Tom Cheasty at centre half-forward split open the Tipperary defence on several occasions and distributed the ball very well. Phil Grimes, playing at left corner forward, scored 1-9 though opposed by John Doyle. Joe Condon dominated the midfield and nullified the efforts of Theo English. Martin Óg Morrissey at centre back was an inspiration to the team and much too good for Mackey McKenna. Jim Irish, who played on Jimmy Doyle, confined him to one score, a goal from play.

In contrast to a fluent Waterford display, Tipperary had many problems. They had difficulty at midfield and centre back. They started with Theo English and Seán English at midfield but finished with Donie Nealon and substitute Tom Moloughney instead. Liam Devaney, who started at full forward, finished up at centre forward. Theo English and Tony Wall finished among the forwards on a day when Tipperary made an unusual number of changes. Roger Mounsey had a poor day between the posts and should have stopped two of the goals.

WATERFORD

P. Flynn

T. Cunningham   A. Flynn   J. Byrne

L. Guinan   M. Óg Morrissey   J. Irish

J. Condon (CAPT.)   M. Dempsey

M. Flannelly   T. Cheasty   F. Walsh

S. Power   J. Barron   P. Grimes

Subs: J. Meaney for M. Dempsey, E. Power for P. Flynn

TIPPERARY

R. Mounsey

John Doyle   M. Maher   K. Carey

M. Burns   A. Wall   M. Murphy

S. English   T. English

Jimmy Doyle   J. McKenna   T. Ryan (KILLENAULE)

D. Nealon   L. Devaney   S. McLoughlin (CAPT.)

Sub: T. Moloughney for S. English

Although Tipperary were Munster and All-Ireland champions and had beaten Waterford well in the previous Munster championship, it was their opponents who were favourites for the Munster final at Limerick on 28 July. Waterford had won the previous two encounters between the sides, which were played with championship fervour. In fact in the league final in May they were clearly the better, the fitter and the more impressive side. They played like a team at the apex of their form, and if Tipperary were holding out any hope of defeating them, it was in the expectation that Waterford might have gone over the top, while they, often finding it hard to get to the peak of form early in the season, might have the edge on this occasion.

Waterford also appeared the more settled side, while Tipperary had doubts about their final selection until close to the game. One new name was included, Pat Ryan of Moycarkey-Borris, who came in at wing back in place of Michael Murphy. Donie Nealon was brought out to centre field to partner Theo English, while Liam Devaney was sent in at full forward to trouble Austin Flynn. Larry Kiely, although thought to be injured, was selected at centre forward in the hope of frustrating Martin Óg Morrissey.

The crowd that turned up for the game in the Gaelic Grounds was a bit of a disappointment at 36,000. According to Deiseach the reason for the small attendance was that the day was too fine for the hurling farmers of the other counties. They had to stay at home for the hay!

When the result of the game was analysed by the local papers the following week, there were two very different conclusions. For Waterford it was 'Hail to our hurling men who, in one tension-charged hour of grim uncompromising battle, took all that Tipperary had to offer and at the end of the struggle fought without quarter, blasted the All-Ireland title holders and emerged the new hurling champions of Munster.' The report continued: 'You may have seen games more spectacular than this . . . but for me this was the greatest victory of them all.'

The Tipperary version was much more sombre: 'The litany of our Limerick sorrows makes formidable reading. Worst of all, a senior defeat in which the scoreboard's grim evidence of a three-point beating was utterly at variance with the trend of play. Tipperary's bid to reverse the league final was eminently successful everywhere except where it mattered. Inaccurate and ill-judged shooting from a well-supplied attack, plus the concession of costly frees in defence robbed Tipperary of a victory which normal form up front would have clinched long before the bitter end.'

The statistics of the game substantiate the Tipperary commentator's chagrin. Tipperary hit seventeen wides to Waterford's ten in the course of the hour. Waterford scored only three points from play, with Philly Grimes getting the remaining eight from placed balls. As Paddy Downey of *The Irish Times* described it: 'Never before did a team dominate a game so completely and with such assured mastery for half an hour and yet find themselves behind at the end.'

Making capital of Waterford's weak midfield, Tipperary controlled virtually every phase of play in the opening half. A lead of ten points in this period would hardly have done justice to the extent of their domination, and yet they had to struggle to stay in front by 0-5 to 0-3 at the interval. The three key Waterford players, Morrissey, Condon and Cheasty, who had dominated the league final, were being kept well under wraps by their respective markers, Kiely, English and Wall.

Waterford faced what little wind there was when the ball was thrown in. After wides on both sides captain, Joe Condon, opened the scoring with a point. Tipperary responded with a beautifully pointed sideline cut from Theo English. The hurling was now fast and furious, the tackling uncompromising. After a few Waterford attacks Cheasty was fouled and Phil Grimes made no mistake with the free, giving Waterford a two points to one lead.

Tipperary won the advantage at centre field and began to increase the supply of ball to the forwards. But the Waterford backs defended well until Donie Nealon sent over to bring the sides level again. Waterford continued to resist the pressure until English pointed to give Tipperary the lead.

Tipperary held the balance of the play midway through the half but were not getting the results their efforts deserved. The forwards, particularly Devaney and Doyle, were hassled by the Waterford backs, and the rewards were meagre. Points by Doyle and Devaney brought Tipperary to a five points to two lead, but it was a poor return for all their efforts. The Waterford backs were playing brilliantly, especially Austin Flynn at full back.

The game continued in this vein until half-time, the intensity of the exchanges reflected in this quotation from one match report: 'A long one dropped to the square where "quarter" was a dirty word. Barron went down hurt. Grimes pointed the free.' The point brought Waterford's tally to three points for the half and the sides went to the dressing rooms with Tipperary leading by 0-5 to 0-3.

It remained anybody's game. The opening minutes of the second half continued with the same intensity. Tipperary attacked with fervour but failed to get through. All the Waterford backs stood like men against the relentless Tipp attack, none more effective than Jim Irish in his policing of Jimmy Doyle. However, Doyle did get a point at the end of these opening minutes to give Tipperary a three-point lead.

At this stage Waterford made a change which was to have an important bearing on the game. Mick Dempsey replaced John Meaney at centre field. Within a very short time he had sent two balls towards the Tipperary square. Grimes pointed one from a resulting free, and Frankie Walsh grabbed the second and sent over the bar to leave only a point between the sides. Dempsey was now rampant and a further delivery resulted in another point from a Grimes free to bring the sides level at six points each.

Waterford were now on top. The Tipperary backs were fouling badly. Another Grimes free was sent to Séamus Power, who pointed. Grimes himself was fouled once again and pointed the free to put Waterford two points ahead. They had now scored five points without reply.

But Tipperary weren't dead yet. They switched frantically to regain the initiative. Devaney went to centre field, McKenna to the 40 and Kiely to full forward. Jimmy Doyle tried for a goal from a close-in free, but it was sent out for a 70. Wall was wide with the shot. Doyle got a point and Kiely followed with another to bring the sides level again at eight all.

The game now moved to a climax. It was frantic, exciting stuff. The exchanges were fierce, almost frightening. Tipperary threw everything into it, but Waterford did not yield. They demonstrated a wonderful spirit and will to win. In one of their attacks on the Tipperary goal, Grimes was fouled once again and punished the opposition.

At the other end the Waterford backs were giving nothing away, defending to the death. Another Waterford attack brought a foul, and Grimes struck between the posts to put two points between the sides. With four minutes to go there was another free to Grimes, and another point, but more importantly they were now three points to the good.

Tipperary made Herculean efforts to bridge the gap, to get a goal in the dying minutes. But they were met with an equally determined spirit and determination and failed, and Waterford survived to win 0-11 to 0-8.

It was a huge victory for the county, their fifth Munster senior title, and sweet revenge for their humiliation the previous year when they lost 5-14 to 2-3 to their victims. It was also a well-deserved success hewn out of huge determination and effort. For Tipperary it was a major shock, even though they had already lost to Waterford in the Oireachtas and the league. The manner of the defeat was equally disappointing. With one of the most potent sets of forwards in the contemporary game, they were able to score only eight points in the course of the hour. And yet they had tried their hearts out, but they had come up against a back line that wasn't prepared to give an inch on the day. It was a salutary lesson that the great can always meet greater on a particular day.

WATERFORD

Ned Power
(Tallow)

Tom Cunningham	*Austin Flynn*	*John Byrne*
(Dungarvan)	(Abbeyside)	(UCC)

Larry Guinan	*Martin Óg Morrissey*	*Jim Irish*
(Mount Sion)	(Mount Sion)	(Erin's Own)

Tom Cheasty   *Frankie Walsh 0-1*
(Ballyduff)   (Mount Sion)

Joe Condon 0-1	*John Meaney*	*Martin Flannelly*
(Erin's Own, capt.)	(Erin's Own)	(Mount Sion)

Séamus Power 0-1	*John Barron*	*Phil Grimes 0-8*
(Mount Sion)	(De la Salle)	(De la Salle)

Subs: Mick Dempsey (Mount Sion), *Charlie Ware* (Erin's Own), *Eddie Walshe* (De la Salle), *Percy Flynn* (Ferrybank), *Michael Walshe* (Mount Sion), *Tony Mansfield* (Abbeyside), *John Kirwan* (Butlerstown)

TIPPERARY

Roger Mounsey
(TOOMEVARA)

John Doyle   *Michael Maher*   *Kieran Carey*
(HOLYCROSS-BALLYCAHILL)   (HOLYCROSS-BALLYCAHILL)   (ROSCREA)

Mick Burns   *Tony Wall*   *Pat Ryan*
(ÉIRE ÓG, NENAGH)   (THURLES SARSFIELDS)   (MOYCARKEY-BORRIS)

Theo English 0-2   *Donie Nealon 0-1*
(MARLFIELD)   (YOUGHALARRA)

Jimmy Doyle 0-3   *Larry Kiely 0-1*   *Tom Ryan*
(THURLES SARSFIELDS)   (GORTNAHOE-GLENGOOLE)   (KILLENAULE)

J. Mackey McKenna   *Liam Devaney 0-1*   *Seán McLoughlin*
(BORRISOKANE)   (BORRISOLEIGH)   (THURLES SARSFIELDS, CAPT.)

Subs: Liam Connolly (FETHARD) *for Tom Ryan, Mick Murphy*
(THURLES SARSFIELDS) *for Mick Burns. Also Matt Hassett*
(TOOMEVARA), *Michael Lonergan* (MOYCARKEY-BORRIS), *Peter*
O'Sullivan (CASHEL KING CORMAC'S), *Tom Moloughney* (KILRUANE-
MACDONAGHS), *Mick Roche* (Carrick Davins)

REFEREE

Gerry Fitzgerald
(LIMERICK)

5

1966: Cork return from the wilderness

Never before had Cork gone for such a long period without winning a Munster senior hurling final. Not since Christy Ring's last-quarter salvo of three goals against Limerick in the 1956 decider had Cork won the provincial decider. One had to go back to the 1930s for a near-comparable period without a title. After the heroics and achievements of the early 1950s, Cork entered a famine period longer than any in their history.

It is difficult to explain why this should have been. One theory is that the county lost a number of brilliant players through emigration and injury round which a winning team might have been built. There were a number of near-misses, particularly in 1957 when, having defeated Tipperary in the semi-final, they lost to

Waterford in the final in which they had to play without the injured Christy Ring. And then there was the heroic tussle with Tipperary in 1960 which they might have won. In the following year bad management resulted in the team being held up on the way to the Gaelic Grounds in Limerick and were anything but well prepared by the time they took the field. Tipperary led by 3-3 to 0-1 at the interval and eventually won by 3-6 to 0-7, but it might have been much different. Then there was the brilliant Tipperary team of the sixties to contend with.

By the time 1966 came along, Cork were hungry for success, having gone for ten years without a Munster final victory. And yet there were no signs that the worm was turning. The famous Christy Ring had departed the hurling scene as a sub in the 1963 championship and Cork had lost the 1964 and 65 finals by a load of goals. Amazingly, this nadir in the county fortunes was to be the preface to unexpected success.

Cork's road to victory commenced with a draw against Clare in the first round of the championship at Limerick on 19 June. Both teams went into this game in the knowledge that the championship was wide open as a result of Limerick's unexpected dismissal of Tipperary in the first round at Cork two weeks previously.

When the hurling year had dawned the question on the minds of hurling followers was, could Tipperary be beaten. They had been beaten by Kilkenny in the league final, the county's first success over Tipperary in a major competition since 1922, but this was regarded as a mere blip in the county's hurling dominance. They came up against Limerick, who were young and unrated and not expected to give the champions much trouble. The Shannonsiders showed themselves a team of fire and dash and Tipperary just couldn't cope with their super-fitness. Outstanding among them was twenty-one-year-old Eamon Cregan, who devastated the Tipperary rearguard, scoring three goals and five points. Further outfield Bernie Hartigan dominated. The final score was 4-12 to 2-9 in favour of Limerick, and the result seemed the end of an era, and the end of the road for some long-established Tipperary players.

For the *Cork Examiner*, Tipperary's defeat was a momentous event: 'Admired, feared, resented because they held hurling in an iron grip, squeezing out the puny challenge of every other county, now like stricken giants, they have fallen.'

So Cork and Clare had a lot to fight for in their first-round game. Cork were the favourites going into the game, especially in the light of suspensions of four key players, Tony Marsh, Paddy McNamara, Jim Woods and Jimmy Cullinane by the Clare County Board for playing without permission in New York, but they faced imminent defeat with three minutes to go and Clare, who had been inspired by Pat Cronin, three points in front. Cork got a free forty yards from the Clare goal and Justin McCarthy took it. He struck it low and, to his own and everyone else's surprise, it went all the way to the Clare net to give Cork a fortunate draw, 3-8 to 3-8.

CORK

Paddy Barry

Pat O'Connor	Tom O'Donoghue	Denis Murphy
Jerry O'Sullivan	Peter Doolan	Pat Fitzgerald
	Con Roche	Tony Connolly
Justin McCarthy	John O'Halloran	Seánie Barry
Colm Sheehan	Donal Sheehan	Patsy Harte

Subs: Denis Riordan for Fitzgerald, Mick Archer for Harte, Gerard McCarthy for Roche

Cork made a few changes for the replay two weeks later. Peter Doolan went to corner back in place of Pat O'Connor; Denis O'Riordan came in at wing back; Gerald McCarthy was placed at wing forward and Charlie McCarthy replaced Patsy Harte on the inside line. These changes combined to make Cork a much stronger outfit than they were in the drawn game, and after the first twenty minutes there was no doubt about the outcome of the game. It attracted a crowd of 31,000 as against just under 19,000 in the drawn match. After that early period Cork came into their own. Three minutes before half-time they led Clare 1-6 to 1-3, were eight points in front at the interval on a scoreline of 2-8 to 1-3, and by nine minutes after the resumption had hammered Clare into submission with a further three goals and a point. They were totally convincing winners by 5-11 to 1-7 at the final whistle. The display of the two newcomers, Seánie Barry (2-6) and Charlie McCarthy

(1-2), had transformed the forward line.

On the same day that Cork were overcoming Clare in the replayed first round, Waterford were disposing of Galway at the same venue in the Munster semi-final. Waterford's victory was decisive in the end, 2-16 to 1-9, but it was a close-run affair until the final quarter. The sides were level at the interval, Waterford 0-7, Galway 1-4, but the latter might have been in front had they not squandered many chances through over-enthusiasm and lack of experience. Galway improved in the third quarter and the game was still very much up for grabs at the end of it, with Waterford leading by two points. But then, as if shaking off a lethargy, Waterford took matters in hand and almost doubled their scoring in the final fifteen minutes while keeping Galway nearly scoreless. The final score was convincing and deserved.

Cork's next game, which attracted a record crowd, was against Limerick in the semi-final at Killarney on 10 July. On a day when the rain, which held off in the first half, poured down in bucketfuls after the interval, Limerick enjoyed the favour of the strong breeze in the first half and were five points in front at the interval. A feature of the game was the way Limerick star, Eamon Cregan, was policed by Cork's Tony Connolly and held to one point in the game. With wind advantage in the second half, Cork were slow to assert their authority, and Limerick were still ahead with eleven minutes to go. But then two goals in the space of a few minutes brought the game within their grasp. The first came from Charlie McCarthy, who pounced on a rebound from the Limerick goal post. This brought the sides level and almost immediately Seánie Barry slipped the Limerick defence to palm the sliotar into the net for a Cork lead. The game still wasn't over and a final Limerick effort for the equalising goal was deflected over the bar by Cork goalkeeper Paddy Barry to leave the score 2-6 to 1-7 at the end.

CORK

Paddy Barry

Peter Doolan   *Tom O'Donoghue*   *Denis Murphy*

Tony Connolly   *Denis O'Riordan*   *Pat Fitzgerald*

Jerry O'Sullivan   *Justin McCarthy*

Seánie Barry   *John O'Halloran*   *Con Roche*

Charlie McCarthy   *Colm Sheehan*   *Gerard McCarthy*

Sub: Donal Sheehan for Con Roche

The scene was set for the Munster final, which was played at Limerick on 24 July. John Bennett returned to the Cork team for the game and the players and management felt confident that this was to be their final. The three games they had already played in the championship had helped them find the winning formula. A great spirit had developed among the players, and to this was added a fierce determination. The team was inspired by a number of veterans: Bennett, Paddy Fitzgerald, Denis Murphy, Denis O'Riordan, Peter Doolan, Gerry O'Sullivan, Tom O'Donoghue and goalkeeper Paddy Barry who had never won a championship.

Waterford, trained by John Keane, made a number of changes both personnel-wise and positional for the final. Departed from the side that defeated Galway were Jimmy Byrne, Duck Whelan, Mick Murphy and John Warren, and their replacements were Mick Gaffney, Mick Walsh, Vinny Connors and Dan Mahon. Mick Walsh came in at centre back in place of John Condon, who moved to centre field and displaced Duck Whelan. Tom Cheasty was selected at full forward, and corner forward J. Kirwan took up his position on the 40. The full forward line was completely new in Vin Connors, Tom Cheasty and Dan Mahon.

Waterford's preparation didn't give the team much hope for the final. There was a one-point victory over a below-strength Wexford in a challenge that gave little cause for exultation, and a Tipperary side minus eleven regulars inflicted a crushing defeat on the side at Dungarvan ten days before the match.

The final itself was a dour, closely contested affair that never rose to any great heights. It will be remembered for the two goals scored by Cork corner forward, John Bennett, and the goal scored by Waterford's Larry Guinan, who travelled almost a hundred yards with the ball on his hurley before smashing it past Paddy Barry. The final score was 4-9 to 2-9 in Cork's favour.

The vital difference between the sides was Cork's three ties in the championship to date which gave them a fitness and cohesion lacking in Waterford, who were still in the throes of team-building as their changed lineout would indicate. The poor following that came to support them seemed to pre-doom them to failure.

The rain which commenced with the game made the field greasy and the sweeping wind made ball control difficult. Cork elected to play against the breeze and the game remained tight and interesting during the first thirty minutes, at the end of which Cork scored a goal and a point to give them a flattering lead of 2-4 to 1-4.

Within twelve minutes of the restart Cork had virtually won the game, opening up what seemed an unassailable gap of ten points. Waterford, however, refused to accept this verdict but had to wait until the twentieth minute for their second goal. An overall lack of incisiveness in the attack left them trailing by five points and this was to become six before the end as Cork got the last score to win 4-9 to 2-9.

The man who tipped the game in favour of Cork was veteran John Bennett, who was recalled to corner forward for the game. These scores came in a four-minute period in the third quarter, when Cork supporters were beginning to wonder at the wisdom of recalling the Blackrock man. His scores were punctuated by a point from Seánie O'Leary to put plenty of daylight between the sides.

Despite playing with the wind, Waterford were at sea in the opening quarter as the changes made did not work out. Mick Walsh was having a torrid time from John O'Halloran at centre back. Waterford lacked the speed and quick delivery of Joe Condon from the defence, and he was lost at midfield. In addition, the experiment of playing Tom Cheasty at full forward was equally unsuccessful and he was changed within nine minutes to the 40. Some time later Mick Walsh went to corner back and Sonny Walsh was brought to centre back. Just before half-time Joe Condon and Hearne switched.

These switches paid off when in the twentieth minute Frankie Walsh, who had scored Waterford's two previous points from frees, flighted the ball into the square and, as Kirwan upset the Cork defence, Vinny Connors popped up to score. This gave Waterford their biggest lead of five points.

But three minutes later, Seánie Barry, who was very dangerous, flashed in a fine goal. A minute later he had levelled and then just as Frankie Walsh put Waterford a point in front again from a free, Charlie McCarthy made his contribution to Cork's win. He doubled on a ball from about thirty yards out just before the interval and whipped it inside the post to give Cork a 2-4 to 1-4 lead.

Cork's two early second-half goals were killer blows for Waterford, especially in the light of their best display in the game in the third quarter. These efforts, however, were thwarted by the vice-like grip of the Cork backs, especially Pat Fitzgerald. Their only reward was a goal by Frankie Guinan after a long run in the twentieth minute of the half.

There was an inevitability about the last period of the game. Cork were on top and were not going to relinquish their control. One of the best displays came from goalkeeper Paddy Barry. In the end they were deserving winners by six points, 4-9 to 2-9, and they regained the Munster title after a ten-year lapse.

It was an emotional occasion for the Leesiders taking their thirtieth provincial title. The vast majority of the spectators were their supporters and they revealed their jubilation and satisfaction in a seething sea of red and white. It had been a long wait to get back to the winner's enclosure and they revelled in the joy of being there once again. The support of this 'Red Horde' was to grow and become an important factor later in Cork's All-Ireland success against Kilkenny.

There were crumbs of comfort for Waterford. While conceding victory to Cork, they were willing to argue that the result might have been different. From their perspective two of Cork's four goals, the second and the fourth, should never have beaten goalkeeper Michael Foley. Also they recalled a second-half point from less that ten yards range by Tom Cheasty when a goal looked an easier proposition. There were also the many thrilling saves by Cork goalkeeper Paddy Barry. Managerial failings were also pointed out, such as the initial posting of Tom Cheasty at full forward, the moving of Tom Hearne from wing back, where he was having a stormer, to centre field during the game, and the taking off of Mickey Walsh.

CORK

Paddy Barry
(St Vincent's)

Peter Doolan	*Tom O'Donoghue*	*Denis Murphy*
(St Finbarr's)	(Sarsfields)	(St Finbarr's)

Tony Connolly   *Denis O'Riordan*   *Pat Fitzgerald*
(St Finbarr's)   (Glen Rovers)   (Midleton)

Mick Waters   *Justin McCarthy 0-1*
(Blackrock)   (Passage)

Seánie Barry 1-6   *John O'Halloran*   *Gerald McCarthy*
(Rathcormac)   (UCC)   (St Finbarr's, capt.)

Charlie McCarthy 1-0 Colm Sheehan 0-1 John Bennett 2-1
(St Finbarr's)   (Éire Óg)   (Blackrock)

Subs: Finbar O'Neill (Glen Rovers), *Jerry O'Sullivan* (Glen Rovers), *Gerry O'Leary* (Blackrock), *Mick Lane* (Glen Rovers), *Donal Sheehan* (Na Piarsaigh), *Paddy O'Connor* (Brian Dillons)

WATERFORD

Michael Foley
(Mount Sion)

Tom Cunningham   *Austin Flynn*   *Sonny Walsh*
(Dungarvan)   (Abbeyside)   (De la Salle)

Michael Gaffney   *Mick Walsh*   *Tom Hearne*
(Ballygunner)   (Mount Sion, capt.)   (Ballygunner)

Joe Condon   *Larry Guinan 1-0*
(Erin's Own)   (Mount Sion)

John Meaney	John Kirwan	Frankie Walsh 0-4
(ERIN'S OWN)	(BUTLERSTOWN)	(MOUNT SION)

Vinny Connors 1-0	Tom Cheasty 0-3	Dan Mahon 0-1
(BALLYGUNNER)	(BALLYDUFF)	(MOUNT SION)

Subs: Duck Whelan (ABBEYSIDE) for Mick Walsh, John Warren (BALLYGUNNER) 0-1 for John Meaney. Others Jimmy Byrne (MOUNT SION), Mick Murphy (ERIN'S OWN), Willie Walsh (DE LA SALLE), Ned Power (DUNGARVAN)

REFEREE
Gerry Fitzgerald
(LIMERICK)

6

1971: The 'wet–dry ball' affair at Killarney

When the 1971 Munster championship came around, Limerick were the form team, having beaten Tipperary in the league final at the Athletic Grounds, Cork. At the same time Cork were the All-Ireland champions, having accounted for Wexford rather easily in a high-scoring All-Ireland, the first eighty-minute final — in all there were forty-two scores on a scoreline of 6-21 to 5-10 — and they were also the previous year's National League winners.

The year will be remembered for the intense rivalry between Limerick and Tipperary. They played each other four times during the year — it would have been five but for Tipperary's withdrawal from the Oireachtas — and Limerick were the victors on three occasions. In the light of the later victory in the All-Ireland, Tipperary supporters tended to forget the defeats and remember the victory over the Limerickmen in the Munster final at Killarney.

Eamon Cregan believes the rivalry had its origins in the fact that they were neighbouring counties, but also because of the many severe defeats Limerick suffered from the great Tipperary teams of the sixties. If the chance ever came, the county would strike back and the opportunity came during these years.

When league activity resumed in February, Tipperary named a panel of twenty-one which included Peter O'Sullivan, Tadhg Murphy, Noel Lane, Willie Ryan, John Kelly, John Gleeson, Tadhg O'Connor, Jim Fogarty, Liam King, Len Gaynor, Mick Roche, P. J. Ryan, Francis Loughnane, John Flanagan, Phil Lowry, Michael Keating, Jimmy Doyle, Jack Ryan, Pat O'Neill, John Carey, Noel O'Dwyer.

Tipperary lost to Cork in their first game, which meant they had to defeat Offaly and Limerick to qualify for a semi-final place in the league. They defeated Offaly but lost to Limerick. This defeat resulted in a play-off with Limerick at Croke Park. The latter gave a brilliant display and got a last-minute goal to win by 2-15 to 1-15. One report described the game thus: 'It was simply tremendous. No harder hurling has been seen in years. The second half was one sustained piece of furious, headlong combat . . .' Tipperary had to play a quarter-final in which they beat Kildare, and they followed that up by beating Cork in the semi-final and qualifed to meet Limerick once again in the final.

This game was played at Cork on 23 May and attracted a crowd of 20,000. A Richie Bennis point from a free in the final moment clinched the result for a Limerick team that had squandered many chances in the opening quarter. At half-time, after playing with the wind in their favour, Tipperary were behind by 3-6 to 2-4. Second-half switches and three replacements, Michael Nolan, Jimmy Doyle and John Gleeson, didn't improve their chances, and they were behind by 3-12 to 3-11 at the final whistle. The one-point defeat flattered Tipperary much more than they deserved. At least three times in the course of the game Limerick should have scored goals, while Tipperary, on the other hand, got a few fortuitous scores in the course of the hour. It was Limerick's first triumph in the competition since 1947.

LIMERICK

Jim Hogan

Tim O'Brien	*Pat Hartigan*	*Jim O'Brien*
Christy Campbell	*Jim O'Donnell*	*Phil Bennis*
John Foley		*Mick Graham*
Richie Bennis	*Bernie Hartigan*	*Mick Grimes*
Eamon Cregan	*Mick Cregan*	*Donal Flynn*

Sub: John Prenderville for Campbell

After all the excitement of the league the championship was eagerly awaited. Limerick opened their campaign with a first-round victory over

Waterford by 3-10 to 2-8 at Cork. They made heavy work of eliminating no-hopers Waterford and bore no resemblance whatever to the side that performed so brilliantly when winning the National League title at the same venue a week earlier. Obviously the celebration of that win had taken its toll. Limerick led 2-6 to 1-3 at the interval, but Waterford had reduced the margin to two points within four minutes of the restart and a surprise result appeared on the cards. However, Limerick rallied. Bernie Hartigan moved to midfield and began to break up Waterford's supremacy in that area. At the same time the forwards clicked into gear with Eamon Cregan and Eamon Grimes revealing some of their usual dynamism. At the end of a dull, lacklustre game, before little more than 5,000 spectators, Limerick came through with five points to spare.

LIMERICK

Jim Hogan

Tony O'Brien   *Pat Hartigan*   *Jim O'Brien*

Eamon Prenderville   *Jim O'Donnell*   *Phil Bennis*

Seán Foley   *Mick Graham*

Ritchie Bennis   *Bernie Hartigan*   *Eamon Grimes*

Donie Flynn   *Mick Cregan*   *Eamon Cregan*

This win qualified Limerick for a tilt at Cork in the

Munster semi-final at Thurles on 4 July. Played in ideal conditions and before a capacity crowd, this was a game of traditional Munster hurling with all the colour, incident and drama one associates with such an encounter. Both sides had the winning of the game, but fortune favoured the league champions and sent their supporters home celebrating their first Munster championship victory over Cork since 1940.

Limerick deserved to win. All through the game they hurled with a drive and determination that Cork matched only for brief periods. They led 0-5 to 0-1 after twelve minutes, allowed Cork to go five points clear by the twenty-fifth minute, and regained the initiative to be back on terms at 1-9 to 2-6 at the interval. The sides were still level at 2-12 each by the twenty-first minute of the second half. At this stage the game was in the balance, but it was Limerick who held their nerve to record a two-point victory, 2-16 to 2-14.

What won the game for Limerick was their fitness and courage, both of which they had in bottomless supply. Also, a number of shrewd switches were made in the course of the game; none more so than that which brought Eamon Cregan from top of the left to centre forward, where he upset the rhythm of his Cork opposite, John Horgan, who had been dominating the area up to then. Mick Graham also benefited from the switch.

LIMERICK

Jim Hogan

Tony O'Brien (CAPT.)   Pat Hartigan   Jim O'Brien

Christy Campbell   Jim O'Donnell   Phil Bennis

Seán Foley   Bernie Hartigan

Ritchie Bennis   Mick Graham   Eamon Grimes

Donie Flynn   Mick Cregan   Eamon Cregan

Sub: Eddie Prenderville for Campbell

Tipperary had a bye into the second semi-final and played Clare at Limerick on 11 July. They won by 1-15 to 3-4 but were not flattered by their margin of victory. Had their attack been at its best, the gap separating the sides at the finish would have been much larger. Tipperary had the breeze in the first half and led by 1-11 to 0-1 at half-time. Clare got two rather soft goals in the second half and a third from a rebound to come within three points of their opponents in the twenty-third minute, but Tipperary held off the challenge to win by five points.

Mick Roche and Noel Lane were outstanding for the winners. The former's return to defence worked like a charm and all those around him oozed with confidence. The new midfield partnership of Séamus Hogan and P. J. Ryan worked well on its debut. However, the Tipperary forwards did not function. With the wind at their backs in the first half and a steady supply of ball, they could register no more than 1-4, the balance of the 1-11 coming from placed balls. When the pressure was on in the second half, John Flanagan, who was always in the thick of things, began to get some results for his efforts. The remainder of the forwards did not impress.

TIPPERARY

Peter O'Sullivan

Noel Lane   *John Kelly*   *John Gleeson*

Tadhg O'Connor   *Mick Roche*   *Len Gaynor*

Séamus Hogan   *P. J. Ryan*

Francis Loughnane   *John Flanagan*   *Noel O'Dwyer*

Paul Byrne   *Michael Babs Keating*   *Roger Ryan*

Sub: Jack Ryan for Byrne

And so to the Munster final. It was expected that Limerick would start favourites and justifiably so in view of their three league wins over Tipperary, particularly the display they gave in the play-off at Croke Park. They had also shown character and determination in overcoming Cork in the semi-final.

Yet within the county, Tipperary were given a good chance to regain the title. The back line had improved beyond all recognition with Mick Roche slotting in as a natural at centre back. At centre field P. J. Ryan and Séamus Hogan looked the ideal combination. It was also believed that the forwards could not be as bad as they had been against Clare, but it was recognised they would have to sharpen up and improve their finishing.

The Munster final was played at Killarney on 25 July, the third senior hurling final to be played at the venue, the previous ones having been in 1892 and 1950. The choice of venue resulted from a failure of Tipperary and Limerick to agree to a home and away arrangement. Over 30,000 spectators witnessed an eighty-minute thriller in heavy showers.

Tipperary made two changes to the team that beat Clare. Paul Byrne and Roger Ryan were replaced in the full forward line by Jimmy Doyle and Dinny Ryan. The latter had been under suspension for twelve months and hadn't been available until the final. Jimmy Doyle had recovered from injury. Limerick stuck with the fifteen that lined out against Cork.

Tipperary looked anything but championship material in the first half as they fumbled their way through forty minutes of hurling that left their supporters in near despair. They bunched, got in one another's way, misplaced passes and mistimed their strokes in a way that clearly suggested they were under tremendous pressure to atone for the three defeats earlier in the year.

At the same time Limerick, roared on by a huge following which greatly outnumbered the Tipperary supporters, were playing hard, methodical hurling and out-running the Tipperary players. They got off to a great start, helped by two rather easy goals and had 2-3 on the board by the ninth minute. Were it not for a similarly easily conceded goal to P. J. Ryan at the other end, Tipperary would have been in dire straits indeed.

Nothing was going right for Tipperary at this stage. Their defence was extended to the full trying to curb the flying Limerick forwards and giving away a lot of frees, which Ritchie Bennis pointed. Centre field was not going well and the inside forward line was getting the wrong type of ball. By half-time they were trailing Limerick 2-10 to 1-7.

But then there was a dramatic turnabout in the second half. It was the result of important remedial surgery by the Tipperary mentors at half-time. Roger Ryan was introduced at full forward in place of Jimmy Doyle, who had failed to get into the game. The height and strength of the Toomevara man made a tremendous difference, and he created the openings for Babs Keating and others to get the scores. Another move was to bring on Liam King for fellow club man Noel Lane, who had experienced a very difficult first half against Eamon Cregan.

As a result of these changes Tipperary erased the six-point half-time deficit and went five points clear during the third quarter. Francis Loughnane had a Tipperary point on the restart, but clearly what was needed was a quick goal. In the fourth minute Babs Keating, now operating at left corner forward, won possession near his own side of the field, worked his way over to the right to make an angle for himself and sent a seemingly harmless shot to Jim Hogan's right. The Limerick goalkeeper looked to have it covered all the way, but somehow the ball slipped through and into the net.

A minute later Keating was in the picture again as Francis Loughnane was downed going through, and the Ballybacon-Grange man belted the twenty-one yard free all the way to the net.

Now Tipperary had a grip on the game that they were never really going to lose, despite the fact that Limerick were to draw level twice again before the finish. The Tipperary half-back line of Tadhg O'Connor, Mick Roche and Len Gaynor came into their own and set up a barrier that the Limerick forwards found well nigh impregnable. Séamus Hogan began to shine at centre field and the forwards began to find the gaps in the Limerick defence.

Dinny Ryan, who switched to the half-forward line at an early stage, won a number of frees by his determined running. Tipperary were now on top but were not getting the scores to go comfortably clear until Dinny Ryan and Babs Keating combined for the latter to score Tipperary's fourth goal. John Flanagan then pointed and Tipperary were five points clear.

However, Limerick were by no means done. They showed great courage in the face of adversity and after Eamon Grimes pointed for them, the same player broke through and took his chance to lash home a great goal that brought Limerick right back into the game. Indeed, it looked all up for Tipperary when, seven minutes from the end, Willie Moore netted for Limerick, only to find that the whistle had gone beforehand for a free, which Ritchie Bennis pointed to equalise at 3-17 to 4-14.

Excitement was at its keenest at this stage, and a puck of the ball could have decided the issue. Fortunately for Tipperary the ball ran for them. Len Gaynor pointed a long-range free to regain the lead for Tipperary, but Ritchie Bennis brought Limerick on terms with three minutes left. Eamon Grimes had a chance for Limerick after this, but he failed and it was John Flanagan who proved Tipperary's match winner when under tremendous pressure he shot the decisive point in the last minute. In the aftermath of victory this point entered the pantheon of greatest scores ever recorded by a Tipperary hurler. The final score was 4-16 to 3-18.

The game will be remembered as one of the most exciting finals in a long time. The closeness of the encounter in the final quarter, the intensity of the struggle, the hard, relentless rather than polished hurling, and the uncertainty of the outcome all combined to leave a lasting impression on all who attended.

Tipperary's elation on their victory was paralleled by Limerick's disappointment. The players had given so much in the struggle, the followers had supported and applauded with such intensity, that there was an enormous gulf between winning and losing. Their disappointment at losing was compounded by the belief that Willie Moore's goal was unjustifiably disallowed. It left them aggrieved. They also resented the 'stunt' Tipperary pulled by changing the ball before Babs Keating struck the twenty-one yard free in the third quarter.

Eamonn Cregan recalls the devastation felt at the

defeat and how, ironically, the shoulder John Flanagan got after collecting the ball, instead of putting him off his shot knocked him into the space required to hit it over the bar for the winning point. He remembers sitting on a seat in Killarney for an age after the match looking at nothing. He does believe, however, that the defeat hardened them for the years to come.

TIPPERARY

Peter O'Sullivan
(CASHEL)

Noel Lane	*John Kelly*	*John Gleeson*
(LORRHA)	(CAPPAWHITE)	(MONEYGALL)

Tadhg O'Connor	*Mick Roche*	*Len Gaynor 0-2*
(ROSCREA, CAPT.)	(CARRICK DAVINS)	(KILRUANE-MACDONAGHS)

Séamus Hogan	*P. J. Ryan 1-0*
(KILDANGAN)	(CARRICK DAVINS)

Francis Loughnane 0-3	*Noel O'Dwyer 0-1*	*John Flanagan 0-5*
(ROSCREA)	(BORRISOLEIGH)	(MOYCARKEY-BORRIS)

Jimmy Doyle 0-1	*Michael Babs Keating 3-4*	*Dinny Ryan*
(THURLES SARSFIELDS)	(BALLYBACON-GRANGE)	(SEÁN TREACY'S)

Subs: Liam King (LORRHA) for Lane, Roger Ryan (TOOMEVARA) for Doyle, Paul Byrne (THURLES SARSFIELDS) for O'Dwyer. Also John O'Donoghue (ARRAVALE ROVERS), Jack Ryan (MONEYGALL), Michael Jones (NEWPORT), Jim Fogarty (MOYNE-TEMPLETUOHY)

LIMERICK

Jim Hogan
(ADARE)

Tony O'Brien	*Pat Hartigan*	*Jim O'Brien*
(PATRICKSWELL, CAPT.)	(SOUTH LIBERTIES)	(BRUREE)

Christy Campbell   *Jim O'Donnell*   *Phil Bennis*
(CLAUGHAUN)   (GARDA CLUB)   (PATRICKSWELL)

Bernie Hartigan 0-1   *Seán Foley*
(OLD CHRISTIANS)   (PATRICKSWELL)

Richie Bennis 0-12   Mick Graham 0-2   Eamon Grimes 1-1
(PATRICKSWELL)   (CLAUGHAUN)   (SOUTH LIBERTIES)

Donie Flynn 1-0   Mick Cregan   Eamon Cregan 1-2
(CAPPAMORE)   (CLAUGHAUN)   (CLAUGHAUN)

Subs: Willie Moore (DOON) *for Flynn, Eddie Prenderville* (FEDAMORE) *for Phil Bennis, Con Shanahan* (CROOM) *for Foley. Also Jim Allis* (DOON), *Frankie Nolan* (PATRICKSWELL), *Dave Bourke* (GARYSPILLANE), *Leonard Enright* (PATRICKSWELL)

REFEREE
Frank Murphy
(CORK)

7

1973: Limerick gain revenge

The rivalry between Limerick and Tipperary continued into 1973. After the four meetings between the sides in 1971, there was a hiatus in 1972 with only one meeting between them in the league on 19 March, which Tipperary won by two points. The counties avoided each other in the championship. Tipperary lost to Cork in a replayed semi-final, while Clare shattered Limerick's ambitions with a shock win at Ennis in the second semi-final.

The sides met three times in the National League in the spring of 1973, each time ending in a draw. In the first of these meetings on 11 February, the final score was Tipperary 2-10, Limerick 3-7. Len Gaynor got two points from 70s in the final three minutes to force the draw. The sides next met in the league semi-final on 15

April. On this occasion it was Limerick who came from behind with two goals in the last five minutes to force a draw at 2-11 each. Two weeks later the replay was at Birr and this also ended in a draw, 1-12 to 2-9. Tipperary had to play with fourteen men for most of the game after John Gleeson was sent off ten minutes into the game. Limerick got their second goal and a draw when a last-minute Seán Foley 70 was whipped to the net by Eamon Cregan. In extra time Tipperary went into a five-point lead, but Limerick came back with three goals to carry them into their fourth successive league final on a scoreline of 5-10 to 3-14.

The draw for the Munster championship kept the teams apart. Tipperary and Waterford were drawn in a first-round game scheduled for Thurles on 20 May, the first meeting between the sides at the venue in a Munster senior hurling championship since 1958. Waterford had a good league campaign, winning the honours in Division II and taking Wexford to a replay in the quarter-final. The latter went on to defeat Limerick convincingly in the final.

A novel feature of the Tipperary team was the selection of Jimmy Doyle in goal. He had played in the position in the All-Ireland minor final of 1954 and his recall, after so many years of brilliant service in the forward line, was due to the departure of existing goalkeeper Tadhg Murphy (Roscrea) to England. The under-21 goalkeeper Owen Walshe (Borrisoleigh) was promoted as sub goalkeeper. Also included in the subs was Mick Roche, who hadn't played since the previous championship. Missing through suspension were Liam King and Babs Keating.

Waterford got off to the perfect start when Jim Greene deflected a great shot to the Tipperary net in the second minute. During the opening quarter Martin Hickey posed big problems for the Tipperary centre back Tadhg O'Connor, as a result of which the Tipperary goal was under constant pressure. However, Waterford did not get the return for their superiority and were only 1-2 to 0-1 in front after ten minutes. Tipperary began to find their feet and with the Waterford inside back line giving away frees, Francis Loughnane, mainly through frees, brought the sides level by the twenty-fourth minute on a scoreline of 0-7 to 1-4. Five minutes later John Flanagan gave Tipperary an interval lead of a point.

Waterford restarted as they had done in the first half and John Kirwan, who had come on as a substitute, goaled from a mêlée after three minutes. Again Tipperary were slow to get going, but by the end of the third quarter they were level at 0-12 to 2-6. Soon after, John Flanagan had two points to put them clear.

Following the introduction of Mick Roche for Séamus Hogan at centre field, the player lobbed in a ball to the square, which Dinny Ryan deflected to the Waterford net. The score gave Tipperary a five-point lead, and while Waterford always stayed within striking distance afterwards, Tipperary were virtually assured of victory. The final score was Tipperary 1-16, Waterford 2-8.

TIPPERARY

Jimmy Doyle

Jim Fogarty   *John Kelly*   *John Gleeson*

Jimmy Crampton   *Tadhg O'Connor*   *Len Gaynor*

P. J. Ryan   *Séamus Hogan*

Francis Loughnane (CAPT.)   *Noel O'Dwyer*   *Jack Ryan*

John Flanagan   *Roger Ryan*   *Dinny Ryan*

Sub: Mick Roche for Hogan

The first of the semi-finals brought Limerick and Clare to battle at Thurles on 24 June. The result was a victory for Limerick by two points on a scoreline of 3-11 to 3-9 and revenge for their defeat at Ennis the previous year. But it was not a victory that Limerick were proud of. Too many of the Limerick players failed to lift their game to the required pitch. Also, goalkeeper Séamus Horgan, who was making his championship debut, had a nightmare between the posts. After they went into the lead by 2-7 to 1-3 during the first half, Limerick seemed to sit back and relax and allowed Clare right back into the game. With only five minutes remaining the sides were level and Limerick were lucky to get two points in the final period to give them victory.

LIMERICK

Séamus Horgan

Willie Moore   Pat Hartigan   Jim O'Brien

Phil Bennis   Seán Foley   Jack O'Dwyer

Ritchie Bennis   Eamon Grimes

Bernie Hartigan   Eamon Cregan   Liam O'Donoghue

Joe McKenna   Mick Dowling   Frankie Nolan

Subs: Jim O'Donnell for O'Dwyer, Jim Allis for Pat Hartigan

Tipperary made a number of changes for their semi-final game with Cork at Limerick on 1 July. Tadhg Murphy was back in goal in place of Jimmy Doyle. Mick Roche was brought in at wing forward in place of Jack Ryan. Also into the forwards came Paul Byrne and Babs Keating in place of Noel O'Dwyer and Dinny Ryan.

Cork brought a strong outfit to Limerick. The game saw the re-emergence of John Horgan at corner back, Donal Clifford at midfield, Willie Walsh at centre field and Pat Moylan on the wing. The inside forward line contained the dangerous trio of Mick Malone, Ray Cummins and Seánie O'Leary.

The story of this game is easily told. With ten minutes to play Cork looked winners all the way, but then in a dramatic turnabout that was completely out of character with what had gone before, Tipperary scored four goals, leaving their supporters jubilant and Cork bewildered.

At half-time Cork turned over with a lead of 1-7 to 1-3, and the lead should have been greater. Tipperary were alarmingly poor. Part of the problem was a partially injured John Kelly, which led to him fouling Ray Cummins. At the other end Babs Keating was making no impression on Brian Murphy. At the start of the second half Mick Roche moved to centre forward and the Tipperary attack improved, but the sustained pressure brought no scores. Instead, Cork scored to go five points in front. With less than ten minutes remaining it looked all up for Tipperary.

But then the game changed dramatically. The ball broke to Paul Byrne, who drove hard at the Cork goal. Paddy Barry half-blocked it, but before he could clear, John Flanagan and Mick Roche rushed in to help it to the net. Tipperary attacked again and got a free. Francis Loughnane only half hit it, but somehow it went all the way to the net and the lead, 3-4 to 1-9, went to Tipperary for the first time. Three minutes later Gerald McCarthy equalised with a Cork free. It looked like a replay. Then Séamus Hogan won on the flank about thirty-five yards out and his lobbing shot went all the way to the Cork net. A minute later Tadhg O'Connor, with a free from the Tipperary defence, lobbed it into the Cork goalmouth and Roger Ryan got his hurley to the bounce for Tipperary's fifth goal. There was no comeback for Cork. Tipperary won 5-4 to 1-10.

TIPPERARY

Tadhg Murphy

Jim Fogarty   *John Kelly*   *John Gleeson*

Jimmy Crampton   *Tadhg O'Connor*   *Len Gaynor*

P. J. Ryan   *Séamus Hogan*

Francis Loughnane (CAPT.) *John Flanagan*   *Mick Roche*

Paul Byrne   *Roger Ryan*   *Babs Keating*

Subs: Jack Ryan for Keating, Dinny Ryan for Flanagan

There was uncertainty about the venue for the final. Killarney was a possibility as in 1971. Cork Athletic Grounds were also in the reckoning. So also was a toss for a home and away agreement. The latter was eventually agreed and Thurles won. The game was played on 29 July, a most beautiful sunny day, before a shirt-sleeved crowd of over 40,000, the size of the crowd reflecting the interest and rivalry between the sides. And the game did not disappoint, turning out to be a thriller with a final score of 6-7 to 2-18 in Limerick's favour.

The result of the game hinged on a 70 in the last minute of the game. Referee Mick Slattery told the taker, Richie Bennis, that it was the last puck of the match. There was a dispute as to whether it was inside or outside the upright. What mattered was the decision of the umpire that it was inside, and this gave Limerick a one-point victory, their first Munster senior hurling title since 1955 and their first win over Tipperary in a final since 1936. Ironically for Tipperary, the ball that created the 70 was going wide when it was touched by the Tipperary goalkeeper!

The game was similar to many between the sides over the previous three years. Whether in league or championship the games produced hurling and excitement of the highest calibre. On this occasion it was no different. There was hard man-to-man hurling, some patches of very fluent play, a bit of needle in the exchanges, and fluctuating fortunes as each side seemed set to take decisive command, only to have the initiative taken from them soon after.

Apart from the last-minute point, the other thing that decided the match in favour of Limerick was their gamble of playing Ned Rea at full forward. Normally a full back, he was placed at the opposite end for a challenge with Waterford before the final because of the absence of Bernie Hartigan. He performed so well, upsetting the opposing full forward line, that he was picked for the position against Tipperary. He was much too strong for Tipperary full back John Kelly and was directly the cause of three Limerick goals, and indirectly the cause of another. In addition, he won several frees in the goal area, and it was surprising that the Tipperary selectors did nothing to curb the man who was making all the room for the other Limerick forwards, especially Frankie Nolan and Eamon Cregan.

Predictably, Limerick opened the game at breakneck speed and from Eamon Grimes's sideline ball Frankie

Nolan flicked their first goal in the third minute. Shortly afterwards Ritchie Bennis drove a twenty-one yard free wide, but in the eleventh minute he made amends when John Kelly fouled Ned Rea, and the Limerick man belted the free to the net. He followed up almost immediately with a point.

Tipperary were in big trouble, but they gradually crept into the game with a string of points, three from Francis Loughnane and one each from Babs Keating and Roger Ryan. But soon after this encouraging response, Limerick countered with their third goal when Mick Dowling touched a long delivery by Grimes to the Tipperary net.

Tipperary kept soldiering away and had further points from Hogan and Keating before Loughnane had their first goal in the twenty-ninth minute after Roger Ryan made the opening following a centre from Mick Roche. Keating pointed again, and Loughnane netted his second goal in the thirty-seventh minute, tapping in a centre from P. J. Ryan. Loughnane pointed two minutes later to give Tipperary an interval lead of 2-9 to 3-2.

Things looked quite bright for Tipperary at this stage. They had played against the breeze and had absorbed the early onslaught from Limerick. It seemed that a Tipperary victory would follow.

Things looked even brighter as Loughnane and Hogan added points in the first three minutes after the resumption. Limerick reshuffled in an attempt to counter Tipperary. Bernie Hartigan was moved to centre field, Seán Foley to centre back and Eamon Grimes to left half-forward. Tom Ryan was brought in at right half-back in place of Jim O'Donnell.

Limerick enjoyed their best spell from the fifth to the thirteenth minute of this half when, in a spell of superiority, they got three goals. First, Frankie Nolan clipped a very smart score off Foley's 70; then when Jimmy Crampton was slow to clear, Ned Rea made the opening for Eamon Cregan to score in the ninth minute; and four minutes later Rea centred well for Cregan to find the net again.

These scores put Limerick 6-3 to 2-13 in front, and the excitement was tremendous. Bennis went for a goal from a twenty-one, but his shot was saved and Tipperary came back with a Loughnane point. Tipperary brought Jack Ryan into the attack, moving Noel O'Dwyer back to wing back in place of Jimmy Crampton. Loughnane and Liam O'Donoghue exchanged points.

Limerick goalkeeper Séamus Horgan saved well from Hogan, and then twice from a shot by John Flanagan and a rebound. Loughnane pointed twice to level for Tipperary in the thirty-fourth minute, and a minute later pointed again for the lead. Tipperary brought in Dinny Ryan for Jack Ryan, but it was Limerick who came back for a Ritchie Bennis equaliser in the thirty-sixth minute.

Limerick attacked again and Tadhg Murphy saved well in the Tipperary goal, but as he was clearing his lines, the backs fouled and Bennis edged Limerick in front once more. The excitement was heart-stopping at this stage as Tipperary surged forward.

Looking for an equaliser, Noel O'Dwyer won possession at right half-back, couldn't strike the ball but kicked it on to John Flanagan, who hit a beautiful point from sixty yards.

A draw seemed inevitable, but then came a throw-in on the right, just inside the Tipperary half. Bennis won possession, sent it on to Nolan whose shot was half-blocked and the return was turned out for a 70 by Tadhg Murphy. The rest is history as Bennis pointed to give Limerick their thirteenth Munster title and a place in the All-Ireland semi-final against London.

While Tipperary claimed they deserved a second chance, it would have been heart-breaking for Limerick to be deprived of success once again after so many years of unrealised promise. The result confirmed what few Tipperary people would concede, that Limerick were marginally but definitely a better team than Tipperary over the previous three years. They had won more often than they had lost in the games during this period. Killarney stood out as the exception that proved the rule.

In fact the 1973 final was the culmination of a number of successes by Limerick teams against Tipperary. Their first breakthrough was in the Munster minor final in 1963. This was followed by success against the Tipperary under-21 side in the Munster semi-final of 1966. Winning a senior final was a logical progression. The earlier victories had given them a belief in themselves and in their ability to compete.

Post-mortems among Tipperary supporters attributed their demise to the weakness of the inside back line which failed to cope with the forceful play of their opponents. There was the added problem in the centre back position, where O'Connor was never in command. There was also the opinion that the Tipperary forwards went for goals, especially in the second half, when points were there for the taking.

Ultimately hurling won on the day. The game was reminiscent of classics of other days. The setting, the bright sunshine, the shirt-sleeved crowd and the packed stadium couldn't have been better, and the game itself was in keeping with the tradition of great Munster finals.

LIMERICK

Séamus Horgan
(Tournafulla)

Willie Moore	*Pat Hartigan*	*Jim O'Brien*
(Doon)	(South Liberties)	(Bruree)

Phil Bennis	*Jim O'Donnell*	*Seán Foley*
(Patrickswell)	(Doon)	(Patrickswell)

Ritchie Bennis 1-5   *Eamon Grimes*
(Patrickswell)   (South Liberties, capt.)

Liam O'Donoghue 0-1	*Mick Dowling 1-0*	*Bernie Hartigan*
(Mungret)	(Kilmallock)	(Old Christians)

Frankie Nolan 2-1	*Ned Rea*	*Eamon Cregan 2-0*
(Patrickswell)	(Effin)	(Claughaun)

Sub: Tom Ryan (Ballybrown) *for O'Donnell. Also Jim Allis* (Doon), *Joe McKenna* (South Liberties), *Paudie Fitzmaurice* (Killeedy), *Andy Dunworth* (Faughs), *Jim Hogan* (Claughaun)

TIPPERARY

Tadhg Murphy
(ROSCREA)

Jim Fogarty	*John Kelly*	*John Gleeson*
(MOYNE-TEMPLETUOHY)	(CAPPAWHITE)	(MONEYGALL)

Jimmy Crampton	*Tadhg O'Connor*	*Len Gaynor*
(ROSCREA)	(ROSCREA)	(KILRUANE-MACDONAGHS)

Séamus Hogan 0-2   *P. J. Ryan*
(KILDANGAN)   (CARRICK DAVINS)

Francis Loughnane 2-10	*Mick Roche*	*Noel O'Dwyer 0-1*
(ROSCREA, CAPT.)	(CARRICK DAVINS)	(BORRISOLEIGH)

John Flanagan 0-1	*Roger Ryan*	*Michael Babs Keating 0-4*
(MOYCARKEY-BORRIS)	(TOOMEVARA)	(BALLYBACON-GRANGE)

Subs: Jack Ryan (MONEYGALL) *for Crampton, Dinny Ryan* (SEÁN TREACY'S) *for Jack Ryan. Also Paul Byrne* (THURLES SARSFIELDS), *Séamus Shinnors* (NEWPORT), *Jimmy Doyle* (THURLES SARSFIELDS), *Martin Esmonde* (MOYNE-TEMPLETUOHY), *Jim Keogh* (SILVERMINES), *Paddy Williams* (KILRUANE-MACDONAGHS)

REFEREE

Mick Slattery
(CLARE)

1978: Clare stymied by Cork

When Cork played the Munster final at Thurles in 1978, they were going for four in a row and playing Clare for the second year running. Clare had shown great improvement since 1976, partly due to a talented bunch of players but also owing to the appointment in October 1976 of Cork star, Justin McCarthy, as coach. McCarthy brought a new dimension to Clare's preparations, speeding up their hurling skills in general. The result was two National League victories as well as two Munster final appearances.

Cork came into the final with two All-Irelands in a row to their credit. However, they had fared so badly in the league they were relegated to Division 1B. In contrast Clare were league champions, having beaten

Kilkenny in the final on 30 April. It was the third time in a row for the sides to meet in the final, Kilkenny winning in 1976 and Clare on the two subsequent occasions. The 1977 victory was particularly pleasing as Clare trailed the Kilkenny men by 0-7 to 0-3 at the interval. They raised their performance in the second half, almost dominated the game and won by 3-10 to 1-10.

Clare's intentions for the year were well and truly proclaimed at the presentation of the cup after the league win. Their captain, Seán Stack, made only a brief mention of the trophy just won. The main thrust of his speech dealt with the forthcoming Munster championship which he said 'is our real objective'.

In fact there was a feeling of expectation in the Clare air that this was to be their year. The retention of the league after the major disappointment of losing the 1977 Munster final was a major boost to their morale. The defeat of Kilkenny for the second year in a row confirmed their credentials for championship honours. There was a general air of optimism as they headed into the championship.

The Munster senior hurling championship commenced at Dungarvan on 4 June when Waterford easily accounted for Kerry by 5-13 to 0-11. The slump in Tipperary's fortunes continued when they went down to Limerick by 1-14 to 0-9 in the other first-round game at Cork a week later. At the Tipperary County Board meeting following the defeat, one delegate said: 'After twenty-seven training sessions this was the most unfit team ever to go out for the county.' An irate supporter, in a letter to the *Tipperary Star*, wrote: 'I was never so disgusted with the performance. I wonder what is the cause and on whose shoulders the blame lies. In my opinion the top officials on the Tipperary board should be forced to resign.'

———⚬⚬⚬———

Cork played Waterford in the first of the semi-finals at Thurles on 27 June. They won easily, 3-17 to 2-8; in fact they devoured Waterford in the process. Their supremacy was absolute and at times in the second half they exposed a yawning gap in standards. Waterford sought some excuse for their defeat in two drastic errors by goalkeeper Steven Curley, who had a nightmare debut, but they never seriously threatened Cork and were a disorganised bunch long before the game finished.

Waterford's woes started early. Cork, having decided to play against the strong wind, attacked early and within two minutes Ray Cummins had the ball in the Waterford net. The Cork half-back line of Dermot McCurtain, John Crowley and Denis Coughlan were in top form and rarely gave the Waterford forwards an opportunity. Even when Waterford scored a goal after fifteen minutes, misfortune followed. Jim Green, the scorer, collided with the goalkeeper while celebrating the event, and ended up in the back of the net. He was forced to retire at half-time with concussion. Cork led at this stage 2-5 to 1-4 and had the wind to look forward to on the resumption. Whatever hope

Waterford might have had of changing the direction of the game evaporated within a minute of the restart when a harmless shot by Tom Cashman went all the way to the Waterford net. It was the end of the road for Steven Curley, who was immediately substituted by former Waterford soccer player, George O'Grady. It also marked the end of the contest for Waterford, who were twelve points in arrears at the final whistle.

CORK

Martin Coleman

Brian Murphy   *Martin O'Doherty*   *John Horgan*

Dermot McCurtain   *John Crowley*   *Denis Coughlan*

Tim Crowley   *Pat Moylan*

Tom Cashman   *Gerard McCarthy* *Jimmy Barry-Murphy,*

Charlie McCarthy (CAPT.)   *Ray Cummins*   *Seánie O'Leary*

Subs: Jimmy Cronin for Coleman, Mick Malone for Cummins, Pat Horgan for Coughlan

Clare and Limerick met in the second semi-final at Thurles on 2 July before a crowd of 25,627 in damp, overcast conditions. Limerick won the toss and elected to play against a strong wind, a decision which did them no favours. They got only one point in the half and trailed by 1-7 to 0-1 at the interval. However, in the context of the strong breeze the nine-point lead did not appear unassailable. The opinion seemed well founded when they reduced the deficit to six points within four minutes of the resumption. But the expectation of victory didn't last long as Clare came right back into the fray with skill and determination.

By the end of the third quarter Clare were back in a commanding position with a lead of 3-10 to 0-5, the chief architect of their revival being Colm Honan, whose darting runs opened up the Limerick defence. Limerick rallied in the final period and three goals by Willie Fitzmaurice raised their hopes as the margin separating the sides was reduced to four points. But Clare's defence withstood the onslaught and they had their fourth goal in the final minute to give them victory by 4-12 to 3-8.

CLARE

Séamus Durack

Jackie O'Gorman   *Jim Power*   *Johnny McMahon*

Ger Loughnane   *Seán Hehir*   *Seán Stack*

Michael Moroney   *Johnny Callinan*

John McNamara   *Noel Casey*   *Colm Honan*

Pat O'Connor   *Martin McKeogh*   *Enda O'Connor*

Sub: Brendan Gilligan for McNamara

And so the scene was set for the Munster final between the All-Ireland champions, Cork, and the National League champions, Clare, a repeat of the previous year's final in which Cork prevailed by 4-15 to 4-10. However, the Clare supporters remembered the game as one they should have won. Cork had got off to a good start when Tim Crowley goaled from a penalty, but Clare hit back with great goals from Noel Casey and Enda O'Connor and raced into a 2-4 to 1-1 lead. It was to be the high point of Clare's endeavour, but their cup of woe started filling when full back Jim Power was sent off for an incident with Ray Cummins just before half-time. Despite playing for nearly forty minutes with fourteen men, Clare were beaten by only five points. The sending off may have contributed to Cork's win, but equally so was the outstanding performance of John Horgan, who adopted a sweeper role from his position at corner back, and the effort of Jimmy Barry-Murphy in the forwards.

Understandably the repeat meeting between the sides was awaited with great interest. Cork made two changes from the side that defeated Waterford. Denis Burns came in at corner back in place of Brian Murphy, and Mick Malone started at corner forward ahead of Seánie O'Leary. Clare lined out with the same fifteen that had done service against Limerick. They were nearly without the services of goalkeeper Séamus Durack. In a puck-about and warm-up at Tulla that morning, Durack was blocking shots from local man, Pat Danagher. The latter wasn't hitting hard enough to suit the goalkeeper, who called for harder and harder shots. Danagher obliged and caught Durack in the eye with a haymaker. The goalkeeper went down in agony and had to have his head stuck into a barrel of water before he recovered!

The final attracted 54,181 spectators to Thurles, the largest crowd for a decider since 1961. The attendance got good value for their money in what proved to be a dour final, spoiled to some extent by the strong end-to-end breeze. Cork had the advantage of the elements in the first half, but their interval lead of 0-5 to 0-3 did not seem nearly enough. It seemed that Clare's hour had come and that they were about to win their first Munster final since 1932. However, Cork rearranged their forces and managed to get a grip on the vital midfield area. Making good use of the wings, they frustrated Clare's attempts to get back on level terms, and at the finish were still two points to the good on a scoreline of 0-13 to 0-11.

Clare opted to play against the breeze in the first half. They did have a number of early scoring opportunities but failed to take them. Rather surprisingly, it took nine minutes for the first score to be registered and this came from Cork after John Horgan pointed an eighty-five metre free. Clare levelled when Michael Moroney pointed from a line ball about thirty yards out.

Cork were awarded a penalty in the twelfth minute after Ray Cummins was held by Jim Power. It started when Séamus Durack brilliantly grabbed a long drive from John Horgan. After losing his hurley, his attempted hand-pass clearance went over the sideline.

From the resultant cut by Tom Cashman, full forward Cummins gained possession and turned inside Power, but the full back was determined not to let his opponent through. Tim Crowley stepped up to take the penalty, for which Durack was flanked by Jim Power and Ger Loughnane. The shot was saved by Durack before being swept away by Power for a 70, which Horgan sent over for a Cork point.

The next score came in the twenty-first minute, the first score from play. It was a beautiful point from Cork midfielder Tom Cashman, who quickly snapped up a loose ball to increase his team's lead. Clare now brought Enda O'Connor to centre forward in a switch with Noel Casey, and with six minutes to go to the interval, they replied with their first score from play by Colm Honan.

Within a minute John Horgan restored Cork's two-point lead when he was again on target from a sixty yard free, but Clare hit back almost immediately and must be considered unlucky not to have scored a goal. Colm Honan got the ball through to Noel Casey, whose shot was just inches over the bar. The only other score in the first half was a Cork point from a 70 from John Horgan, which left Cork in the lead at the interval by two points, 0-5 to 0-3.

The buzz in the crowd during the interval was expectant. Clare were looking good, having restricted Cork to such a small score, and they had the wind in their favour in the second half. It seemed as though the county was on the threshold of making an important breakthrough.

Cork resumed in the second half with a number of positional switches. Pat Moylan was now at midfield, Tim Crowley at right half-forward; Jimmy Barry-Murphy had gone back to the 40 while Gerald McCarthy was now at left half-forward.

Only two minutes had elapsed before Cork opened the scoring when Charlie McCarthy pointed from a twenty metre free. Clare replied quickly when from a puck-out Enda O'Connor fielded brilliantly and shot over the bar.

Cork substituted Eamonn O'Donoghue for Mick Malone and by the twelfth minute of the half they had increased their lead to five points after Charlie McCarthy pointed twice from frees and Ray Cummins scored another from near the touchline. Indeed Cummins was rather lucky to get away with the score as he had committed a foul by turning twice with the ball before shooting.

Seán Hehir believes that this poor Clare beginning to the second half was due to a decision taken in the dressing room at half-time that the Clare back men were to follow their men if they switched. This was done following the Cork changes at the interval, and he believes it resulted in a loss of cohesion among the backs. Before they had readjusted Cork had gone into a five-point lead, and Clare were chasing the game for the rest of the half.

Clare came back with two points from Colm Honan to leave them trailing by just three points with twenty minutes remaining. Charlie McCarthy and Honan exchanged points with the Clare score coming from a free awarded following a late foul on Loughnane.

At this stage Clare introduced Brendan Gilligan at full forward for Martin McKeogh, but it was Cork who continued to dominate and they restored their five-point lead with scores from Tim Crowley and Ray Cummins. With ten minutes remaining Honan pulled one back for Clare before Séamus Durack made a brilliant save from Tim Crowley. Cork introduced Pat Horgan for Pat Moylan at this point, and with six minutes remaining there were again only three points between the sides after Johnny Callinan pointed.

With less than three minutes to go Colm Honan pointed to reduce the leeway to just two points. Indeed his decision to take a point from this free was to be a talking point, as many felt that Clare should have tried to engineer a goal from the free. However, Honan was seen to signal to coach, Justin McCarthy, and the result was that he shot for a point.

From the puck-out Tom Cashman gained possession and raced away before being awarded a free, the referee deeming him to have been fouled by Jackie O'Gorman. Charlie McCarthy pointed. Cork attacked again from the puck-out, but Séamus Durack again saved before carrying the ball to midfield in an attempt to raise his side to one last attempt. At midfield he passed to Ger Loughnane whose attempted lob into the Cork square went that little bit too far and went just over the bar. Indeed there were those who felt that Clare were unlucky not to have been awarded a twenty metre free at this point, as Loughnane was tackled after hitting the ball. After the puck-out the final whistle sounded and

Clare had again failed when they most needed to win. The final score was 0-13 to 0-11 in Cork's favour, which gave them their thirty-seventh Munster senior hurling title and their first four in a row since 1926–29.

It was a strange final with both teams playing well below par. The Clare supporters remember the frustration of watching so many of their forwards not performing, but they forget that the Cork players were under-performing also. It was a game controlled by the backs and no mistakes were made by either side. The final scoreline had an unreal look about it. Cork got nine of their thirteen points from frees. When before or since did Cork win a Munster final scoring only four points from play? Clare scored only six points from play, which wasn't much better.

Seán Hehir is inclined to remember the game in comparison with the 1977 final. They had learned a lot from that defeat and were better prepared for the 1978 encounter. Unfortunately the Clare forward line did not reach the brilliance of their performance the previous year, just as the backs in 1977 never reached the performance level of the following year. Looking back, success for Clare would have come had they been able to marry the forward performance of 1977 with the defence of 1978.

Hehir has another interesting point to make. He believes Cork were focused in a very special way for the final. In conversations with Cork players in after-years, he learned that Cork did not take kindly to a Corkman helping Clare. He might help out Antrim or some other team, but not their immediate opposition. They were not going to tolerate defeat at the hands of a Clare team trained by Justin McCarthy.

Ultimately, it must have been the superior experience of Cork that contributed to their victory. They had won two All-Irelands in a row and were going for their thirty-seventh provincial title. They hadn't been beaten by Clare in a Munster championship game since 1955. They had the confidence therefore that came from so much experience and so many wins. Clare, by contrast, were striking into the unknown. They hadn't won a provincial decider since 1932. They had lost so often it was difficult for them to make the psychological leap into a winning mode.

Séamus Durack believes that the failure to win in 1977 was the real disaster. He recalls two incidents which changed the direction of that game. One was the decision to let a goal by Ray Cummins stand after he had fouled the ball, when Clare were five points up. Instead of the goal being allowed, Clare should have been awarded a free which they should have been hitting from twenty-five yards out right down into the Cork goal. The second incident was the sending off of Jim Power for something the referee didn't see, in contrast to his total failure to see a foul on Power sometime previously by a Cork forward. He is convinced Clare would have won otherwise and that the defeat set back Clare hurling enormously. In 1978 the level of expectancy on the shoulders of the Clare team was so great that many of the players froze on the day. On a personal note, he doesn't like talking about the defeat because all he felt after it was 'utter, absolute despair and disappointment'.

Justin McCarthy's comment on the defeat was interesting: 'There was too much of a continuation from the league to the championship. There should have been a break and there should not have been so much physical training. It stemmed probably from the lack of success. They just needed to keep ticking over; a lot of the team were tired.'

CORK

Martin Coleman
(Ballinhassig)

Denis Burns	*Martin O'Doherty*	*John Horgan 0-4*
(St Finbarr's)	(Glen Rovers)	(Blackrock)

Dermot McCurtain	*John Crowley*	*Denis Coughlan*
(Blackrock)	(Bishopstown)	(Glen Rovers)

Tom Cashman 0-1   *Tim Crowley 0-1*
(Blackrock)   (Newcestown)

Gerard McCarthy	*Jimmy Barry-Murphy*	*Pat Moylan*
(St Finbarr's)	(St Finbarr's)	(Blackrock)

Charlie McCarthy 0-5	*Ray Cummins 0-2*	*Mick Malone*
(St Finbarr's, capt.)	(Blackrock)	(Éire Óg)

Subs: Eamonn O'Donoghue (Blackrock) *for Malone, Pat Horgan* (Glen Rovers) *for Moylan. Also Brian Murphy* (Nemo Rangers), *Seánie O'Leary* (Youghal), *John Allen* (St Finbarr's), *John Fenton* (Midleton), *Jerry Cronin* (Newmarket), *Pat McDonnell* (Inniscarra), *Donal O'Grady* (St Finbarr's), *John Buckley* (Glen Rovers)

CLARE

Séamus Durack
(Feakle)

Jackie O'Gorman	*Jim Power*	*Johnny McMahon*
(Cratloe)	*(Tulla)*	*(Newmarket)*

Ger Loughnane 0-1   *Seán Hehir*   *Seán Stack*
(Feakle)   *(O'Callaghan's Mills)* *(Sixmilebridge, capt.)*

Michael Moroney 0-1   *Johnny Callinan 0-1*
(Crusheen)   *(Clarecastle)*

Jimmy McNamara   *Noel Casey 0-1*   *Colm Honan 0-6*
(Newmarket)   *(Sixmilebridge)*   *(Clonlara)*

Pat O'Connor   *Martin McKeogh*   *Enda O'Connor 0-1*
(Tubber)   *(O'Callaghan's Mills)*   *(Tubber)*

Sub: Brendan Gilligan (Éire Óg) for McKeogh. Also Pat Morey (Sixmilebridge), Tommy Keane (Kilmaley), Michael O'Connor (Parteen), Mickey Murphy (Clooney), Con McGuinness (Feakle), Gerry Nugent (Scarriff), Flan McInerney (Sixmilebridge), Barry Smythe (Éire Óg), Tom Glynn (Éire Óg)

REFEREE

John Moloney
(Tipperary)

1980: Limerick halt Cork's gallop

When the Munster championship got under way in 1980, Cork were going for an unprecedented six senior titles in a row, and looked likely to succeed. They had beaten Limerick comprehensively in the replay of the National League final at Cork on 18 May. The sides had drawn two weeks previously when Ollie O'Connor rescued Limerick with a spectacular goal in the closing seconds. Limerick continued to match their opponents for about forty minutes of the replay, but after that Cork took over and were convincing winners by 4-15 to 4-6 at the final whistle.

Why the replay was played at Cork rather than Limerick is unclear. Limerick felt they were wronged and defeat aggravated their grievance. They were determined on revenge and when they qualified for the Munster final later in the year, they had huge motivation. They were not going to lose the final.

Clare and Waterford were drawn in the first round at Thurles on 1 June. In an entertaining game the Claremen survived a strong Waterford challenge to win by 3-13 to 2-11. Clare had gone into the game as favourites but were by no means impressive. While they started well they weren't sure of a semi-final spot until a second goal midway through the second half put them back in front. Clare were without the leadership of team captain Noel Casey in attack and lost the services of centre back Ger Loughnane through injury after nineteen minutes. That having been said, the team performance was well back on what they had produced in the Munster finals of 1977 and 78.

Clare continued to disappoint against Limerick in the semi-final at the Gaelic Grounds two weeks later, going down 3-13 to 2-9. Limerick were much sharper in their approach work and their ability to capitalise on opportunities. In stark contrast, Clare failed dismally again and again to convert possession into scores. If Clare had managed to put away some of the gilt-edged chances which fell into their path, the result could have been different.

Clare opened well and had 1-2 on the board to Limerick's two points within seven minutes. But a Limerick save from a Noel Casey blockbuster a minute later seemed to knock them back in their tracks, and they didn't score again until five minutes before the interval. Limerick in the meantime had taken over, and great performances by Leonard Enright at full back and Seán Foley on the wing halted Clare's scoring attempts. At the other end of the field Eamon Cregan, Ollie O'Connor, Joe McKenna and Willie Fitzmaurice gave the Clare backs a torrid time. From three points down Limerick went five points in front.

Clare got a major boost in the thirtieth minute when Enda O'Connor tapped in a goal after the ball from his shot rebounded off Tommy Quaid in the Limerick goal. While this score was a major psychological boost to Clare, its effect was offset just before half-time when Eamon Cregan blasted a penalty to the net to leave Limerick leading 2-7 to 2-2 at the interval.

On the resumption Clare trimmed the Limerick lead by two points, but when the need of a goal was greatest, Enda O'Connor and Noel Ryan sent two glorious chances wide. In fact squandermania was to be Clare's lot during the half. The backs played well but when the ball went to the forwards, opportunities were not converted. At the same time the Limerick forwards made the most of fewer chances. They went six points in front, but Clare pegged back the lead to four before Eamon Cregan had a goal and a point in the last seven minutes to give Limerick an undisputed victory by 3-13 to 2-9.

LIMERICK

Tommy Quaid

Donal Murray   *Leonard Enright*   *Dom Punch*

Paudie Fitzmaurice   *Mossy Carroll*   *Seán Foley* (CAPT.)

Jimmy Carroll   *David Punch*

Liam O'Donoghue   *John Flanagan*   *Willie Fitzmaurice*

Ollie O'Connor   *Joe McKenna*   *Eamon Cregan*

Sub: Eamon Grimes for Flanagan

The second semi-final, between Cork and Tipperary, was played at Thurles on 22 June. Cork had no difficulty in defeating a spiritless Tipperary side on a day that saw the reopening of a newly vamped Semple Stadium. Over 42,000 spectators turned up to see Tipperary suffer yet another championship defeat and continue to languish in the hurling doldrums.

Before the game there were doubts about the Tipperary centre field pair and the forward line, but the day proved the team had defensive flaws as well. Because the team didn't work from the start, the players were moved about to try and find a winning combination. By the end of the game only the goalkeeper and the inside backs held their original positions. However, the changes had no effect. Although they had the wind in the first half, Tipperary trailed by 1-6 to 0-6 at the interval. At no stage were they in control of the game and were lucky not to be more than eight points in arrears at the final whistle on a scoreline of 2-17 to 1-12. So superior were Cork in all facets of play that one was left reflecting at the end on the alarming gap in standards which existed between the sides.

The hurling Cork played was straight from the expert's handbook. Their defence did a magnificent job of curtailment when playing against the strong breeze and rain which blew into their faces in the first half, and their forwards displayed imaginative attacking hurling when aided by the elements in the second half.

Having chosen to play with the help of the breeze in the opening half in the hope of having a cushion of scores when they faced into it after the interval, Tipperary were stymied from the word go by a Cork back line that never allowed them to settle and gave them few opportunities to score. Brian Murphy, Martin O'Doherty, John Crowley and Dermot McCurtain were dominant figures in that defence. Instead of having a cushion, they trailed Cork 1-6 to 0-6 at the interval, and the margin would have been greater had Cork not hit twelve wides during that period.

There was very little change in the second half with the exception of a five-minute period early on when Tipperary put in a much-improved performance and reduced the Cork lead to two points. But Cork rearranged their team and within three minutes Tom Cashman had the ball in the Tipperary net. This score sounded the death-knell for Tipperary and rarely again did they seriously challenge the might of Cork. In the

1. *A dramatic interception by Mossie O'Riordan (Cork) flicks the sliotar past Tony Reddin (Tipperary) in the 1952 Munster final at Limerick.*

2. *A battered and bruised Christy Ring (Cork) after the 1952 Munster final between Cork and Tipperary at Limerick.* (Cork Examiner)

3. Lorrha and Tipperary hurling stars of the past, Tony Reddin and Liam King, at the opening of St Ruadhan's pitch and club facilities at Lorrha on 13 June 1993.

CRAOḃ IOmÁNA   NA mumAN

AN CLÁR

— v. —

Luimneaċ

ı Luimneaċ

ᴅIA ᴅomnaIʒ 10Aᴅ IúIL, 1955.

CLÁR OIFIʒeAmAIL

LUAċ - - -   6p.

4. Front cover of the match programme for the 1955 Munster final at Limerick.

5. *The Clare team that defeated Cork in the first round of the 1955 Munster championship. The team showed one change for the Munster final, with Tom Fahy replacing Johnny Purcell.* BACK ROW (LEFT TO RIGHT): *M. Hayes, W. Stritch, J. Smyth, D. Sheedy, D. Dillon, J. Purcell, N. Deasy.* FRONT ROW (LEFT TO RIGHT): *J. Carney, M. Nugent (capt.), J. Ryan, M. Leahy, D. O'Grady, J. Greene, D. McInerney, H. Donnellan.*

6. *Mick Mackey (trainer) with members of the Limerick team preparing for the 1955 Munster final.* (LEFT TO RIGHT): *Jack Quaid, S. Leonard, Jim Quaid, M. Mackey, L. Ryan (capt.), D. Broderick, E. Noonan, R. Prendergast, S. Ryan, A. Raleigh, D. Kelly, G. Fitzgerald, P. O'Malley.*

7. *The Limerick team that sensationally defeated Clare in the 1955 Munster final.* BACK ROW (LEFT TO RIGHT): *Mick Mackey (trainer), J. Keogh, T. Casey, Jim Quaid, S. Ryan, Jack Quaid, S. Leonard, R. Prendergast, D. Kelly, Jimmy Butler Coffey (former Tipperary All-Ireland player).* FRONT ROW (LEFT TO RIGHT): *P. Cunneen, D. Broderick, P. Enright, E. Noonan, L. Ryan (capt.), V. Cobbe, G. Fitzgerald.*

8. *Dr Thomas Morris, Archbishop of Cashel, throwing in the ball for the first time as Patron of the GAA, at the start of the 1960 Munster final between Cork and Tipperary at Limerick.*

9. The Tipperary team that defeated Cork in the 1960 Munster final at Limerick. BACK ROW (LEFT TO RIGHT): M. Maher, John Doyle, S. McLoughlin, K. Carey, L. Moloughney, L. Devaney. FRONT ROW (LEFT TO RIGHT): T. Ryan, T. English, T. Moloney, L. Connolly, T. Wall (capt.), D. Nealon, M. Burns, M. Hassett, Jimmy Doyle.

10. Waterford goalkeeper Ned Power making a dramatic catch before clearing the sliotar in the 1959 Munster final against Cork.

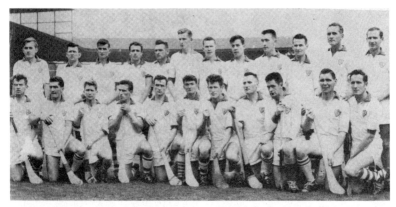

11. *The Waterford panel in the 1963 championship.* BACK ROW (LEFT TO RIGHT): *J. Barron, P. Flynn, E. Walshe, M. Dempsey, A. Flynn, J. Kirwan, J. Meaney, J. Byrne, J. McGrath, F. Walsh, P. Grimes, C. Ware.* FRONT ROW (LEFT TO RIGHT): *T. Cunningham, M. Óg Morrissey, M. Flannelly, L. Guinan, J. Condon (capt.), J. Irish, T. Cheasty, S. Power, T. Mansfield, M. Walshe, N. Power.*

12. *Tipperary players and mentors before a 1960s National League game.* (LEFT TO RIGHT): *John Doyle, Paddy Leahy, Michael Maher and Martin Kennedy.*

13. *The Cork senior hurling panel in 1966.* BACK ROW (LEFT TO RIGHT): *J. Barrett (county chairman), D. Murphy, T. O'Donoghue, J. O'Halloran, A. Connolly, P. Doolan, M. Waters, J. McCarthy, P. Fitzgerald, D. Sheehan, J. Bennett, J. Barry (trainer).* FRONT ROW (LEFT TO RIGHT): *G. O'Sullivan, C. Sheehan, P. Barry, C. McCarthy, G. McCarthy (capt.), S. Barry, F. O'Neill, G. O'Leary.*

14. *The Tipperary team that defeated Limerick in the 1971 Munster final.* BACK ROW (LEFT TO RIGHT): *Ossie Bennett (masseur), Noel Lane, Noel O'Dwyer, Mick Roche, Seamus Hogan, John Kelly, Michael 'Babs' Keating, John Gleeson, Gerry Doyle.* FRONT ROW (LEFT TO RIGHT): *Peter O'Sullivan, Len Gaynor, P. J. Ryan, Tadgh O'Connor (capt.), Jimmy Doyle, John Flanagan, Dinny Ryan, Francis Loughnane.*

15. Tadhg O'Connor, Tipperary captain, making a speech after the defeat of Kilkenny in the 1971 All-Ireland final.

16. *Tipperary players Len Gaynor and Seamus Hogan look on anxiously as a Limerick forward gains possession in the 1973 Munster final at Thurles.* (CORK EXAMINER)

17. *Ray Cummins (Cork) about to strike the ball despite the attentions of John Kelly and Seamus Hogan (Tipperary), with Pat Moylan (Cork) running parallel, in the 1973 Munster semi-final between Cork and Tipperary.*

18. *The Cork team led by captain Charlie McCarthy parade before the 1978 Munster final at Thurles.* (CORK EXAMINER)

19. *The Clare team that lost to Cork in the 1977 Munster final. There was only one change for the 1978 final. Gus Lohan had retired and Martin McKeogh (O'Callaghan's Mills) had come into the team.* BACK ROW (LEFT TO RIGHT): *S. Stack, G. Loughnane, E. O'Connor, J. O'Gorman, J. Power, G. Lohan, S. Hehir, N. Casey.* FRONT ROW (LEFT TO RIGHT): *C. Honan, P. O'Connor, J. Callanan, S. Durack, J. McNamara (capt.), M. Moroney, J. McMahon.* (CLARE EXPRESS)

20. Eamon Grimes (Limerick) in action in the 1980 Munster championship. (SPORTSFILE)

21. *Joe McKenna, a major force in the Limerick forward line during the 1980 championship.*
(SPORTSFILE)

22. *The Limerick team that defeated Clare in the 1981 Munster final at Thurles.* BACK ROW (LEFT TO RIGHT): *J. McKenna, P. Kelly, D. Punch, L. Enright, E. Cregan, T. Quaid, J. Flanagan.* FRONT ROW (LEFT TO RIGHT): *L. O'Donoghue, S. Foley, J. Carroll, M. Grimes, P. Fitzmaurice, B. Carroll, P. Herbert, O. O'Connor.*

23. *Action from the 1981 Munster senior hurling final, between Joe McKenna (Limerick) and Ger Loughnane (Clare).* (CORK EXAMINER)

24. *Cork captain John Fenton is mobbed by his fans after victory in the 1984 Munster final against Tipperary.* (INPHO)

25. *Action from the 1984 Munster final: John McIntyre (Tipperary), Tim Crowley and Kevin Hennessy (Cork) contest for the ball.* (INPHO)

26. *Intense exchanges in the 1984 Munster final as Denis Mulcahy (left) and John Blake (Cork) try to dispossess Noel O'Dwyer (Tipperary).* (INPHO)

27. *A study in concentration as the hurling pack pursues the sliotar in the 1984 Munster final between Cork and Tipperary.* (LEFT TO RIGHT): *John Crowley (Cork), John Hodgins (Cork), Michael Doyle (Tipperary), Pat Hartnett (Cork), Dermot McCurtain (Cork).* (CORK EXAMINER)

end the score was 2-17 to 1-12 in Cork's favour, the eight-point margin of defeat flattering the Tipperary effort.

CORK

Timmy Murphy

Brian Murphy   Martin O'Doherty   John Horgan

Denis Coughlan   John Crowley   Dermot McCurtain (CAPT.)

John Fenton   Tom Cashman

Jimmy Barry-Murphy   Pat Horgan   Tim Crowley

Seánie O'Leary   Brendan Cummins   Eamonn O'Donoghue

Cork and Limerick lined out in the Munster final at Thurles before 43,090 spectators on 20 July with the same teams that won the semi-finals. Cork made positional changes in the half-forward line with Jimmy Barry-Murphy and Tim Crowley changing wings. Limerick hadn't defeated Cork in a Munster championship game for nine years or in a Munster final since 1940.

Playing with the wind in the first half, Limerick had the best possible start when, after Cork goalkeeper Timmy Murphy dropped a shot from Limerick midfielder Jimmy Carroll, Eamon Cregan finished it to the net. Soon after, the same player added a point from a free.

It was to be a long time before Limerick got their next score. Cork drew level in the twelfth minute when Pat Horgan dispossessed Leonard Enright in the left corner and crossed to Eamonn O'Donoghue, who goaled. Cork were now doing well in their half-forward line, but Limerick were holding out firmly in the inside back line. Cork were also guilty of inaccuracy and by half-time had a tally of ten wides.

Limerick meanwhile hadn't scored since the opening period. They nearly scored a second goal in the twenty-first minute following a second error from Timmy Murphy but had to make do with a point from David Punch three minutes later, their first score in nineteen minutes. They improved around the field and were getting on top as they approached half-time. They opened up a five-point lead, which was reduced to four by an Eamonn O'Donoghue point just before the interval, leaving the half-time score Limerick 1-7, Cork 1-3.

With the benefit of the wind Cork began the second half impressively with a Pat Horgan point which he kicked over the bar after only ten seconds and a Fenton free five minutes later to narrow the gap to two points. Significantly this was to be the nearest Cork ever came to wiping out the deficit.

The first real sign of a Limerick takeover came when Cregan pointed two frees — the result of ever-increasing pressure on the Cork backs — and when David Punch hit over a great score from the left wing in the forty-fifth minute.

However, Cork hit back with a typical goal. Barry-

Murphy won possession from the puck-out, forced his way past several defenders and then set up Seánie O'Leary for the score. Two points once more separated the teams, and that was the way it stayed during a period of uncertainty for both sides until the deadlock was broken with nineteen minutes remaining.

Donal Murray landed a free about thirty yards out on the right wing. Horgan and O'Doherty went for the ball, clashed and, unchallenged, Ollie O'Connor raced away before goaling with a powerful low shot. It extended Limerick's lead to five points once more, but more importantly it marked the turning point for the team. The score gave Limerick a powerful, psychological lift. They showed greater commitment as if they felt now that the game was theirs. They also improved their performance with inspired displays from Liam O'Donoghue at half-back, David Punch and Jimmy Carroll at centre field, and the unorthodox Willie Fitzmaurice at left half-forward.

Cork lost ground around the centre of the field after Cashman was switched to right half-forward, with Tim Crowley moving out. However, after a short time Cashman was moved again to wing back in place of McCurtain, with substitute Pat Moylan filling the gap in attack. McCurtain, injured in a heavy tackle in the fifteenth minute, had been fairly effective for most of the first half, but for ten minutes after the resumption he was totally out of touch. Cashman did hurl well at half-back, but Tim Crowley did not benefit from the change and Moylan brought no improvement even though he did win possession.

With Johnny Crowley having faded and Denis Coughlan well beaten, though he had been in command earlier on, the absence of McCurtain was felt all the more. It meant that with Limerick on top at midfield, Cork were under so much pressure that an ailing attack got nothing like the support it needed. The inside Cork line of Brian Murphy, Martin O'Doherty and John Horgan remained sound.

Up front Jimmy Barry-Murphy and Eamonn O'Donoghue were best of the forwards and Cork's best chance of saving the day. Points by Tim Crowley and John Fenton reduced the margin to a goal by the fifty-fifth minute, but lost opportunities proved costly.

With the game entering the final ten minutes and the title appearing within their grasp, Limerick were able to increase the pressure. Willie Fitzmaurice's opportunism won him a point after he picked up a short clearance from the Cork goalkeeper. This was cancelled out by a Fenton point from a sixty-first minute free, but two further Cregan points saw Limerick insulated against any late rally with a five-point advantage.

And so time ran out and any Cork recovery was stymied by the heroic work of the Limerick defence, especially Enright at full back and captain, Seán Foley, on the wing. At the other end Liam O'Donoghue was magnificent.

Charlie McCarthy, who was introduced for Cork with ten minutes remaining, had no better luck than Pat Moylan. McCarthy came in for Ray Cummins who, in line for a twelfth successive provincial medal, was obviously affected by his three-week spell in the US, where he was unable to train.

For a change, in the closing stages luck was on Limerick's side as a low ball from Barry-Murphy was deflected out for a 70. Then the same player made an opening for O'Leary, which promised a goal until the ball came back off the keeper. Shortly after, Fenton, after receiving from Barry-Murphy, rifled a close-in shot over the bar when it seemed easier to put the ball in the net.

After that there was no way Limerick could lose, and they had four points to spare on a scoreline of 2-14 to 2-10 when the final whistle sounded.

For Limerick it was a long overdue triumph, wiping out the memories of a succession of major defeats by Cork, the most recent in the league final replay, and providing a straight passage to the All-Ireland final for the first time since 1974. It was a success based on an absolute conviction in their own ability matched by a craving for victory. They had their luck also, an ingredient that had deserted them on numerous occasions in the past.

Eamon Cregan gives centre forward John Flanagan great credit for the victory. He was a very stong player, one you'd want playing for you rather than against you, and his rugged style and determination upset the Cork half-back line and prevented them from getting into their rhythm.

For Cork there was the disappointment of defeat and the failure to achieve the historic six in a row. There was also the feeling that they had let it slip. They seemed strongly placed for a win when facing the second half four points down but with a strong wind behind them. Yet, against the run of play, it was Limerick who dictated the game, gaining inspiration from a vital Ollie O'Connor goal in the fifty-first minute and ultimately taking control with a powerful fifteen-man effort in which their defence played a major role.

LIMERICK

Tommy Quaid
(FEOHANAGH)

Donal Murray   *Leonard Enright*   *Dom Punch*
(CROOM)   (PATRICKSWELL)   (PATRICKSWELL)

Paudie Fitzmaurice   *Mossy Carroll*   *Seán Foley 0-1*
(KILLEEDY)   (GARRYSPILLANE)   (PATRICKSWELL, CAPT.)

Jimmy Carroll 0-1   *David Punch 0-2*
(GARYSPILLANE)   (PATRICKSWELL)

Liam O'Donoghue 0-1   *John Flanagan*   *Willie Fitzmaurice 0-1*
(MUNGRET)   (FEOHANAGH)   (KILLEEDY)

Ollie O'Connor 1-1   *Joe McKenna 0-1*   *Eamon Cregan 1-6*
(BALLYBROWN)   (SOUTH LIBERTIES)   (CLAUGHAUN)

Subs: Séamus O'Sullivan (TOURNAFULLA), *Eamonn Grimes* (SOUTH LIBERTIES), *Paddy Kelly* (KILMALLOCK), *Brian Carroll* (GARRYSPILLANE), *Pat Foley* (PATRICKSWELL), *Ger Mulcahy* (DROMIN ATHLACCA), *Con O'Keeffe* (BALLINGARRY), *Mike Grimes* (SOUTH LIBERTIES)

SELECTORS

Noel Drumgoole, J. P. Ryan, Tony O'Brien, Tim Horgan, Vincent Byrnes

CORK
Timmy Murphy
(BLACKROCK)

Brian Murphy   *Martin O'Doherty*   *John Horgan*
(GLEN ROVERS)   (GLEN ROVERS)   (GLEN ROVERS)

Denis Coughlan 0-1   *John Crowley*   *Dermot McCurtain*
(GLEN ROVERS)   (BISHOPSTOWN)   (BLACKROCK, CAPT.)

John Fenton 0-6   *Tom Cashman*
(MIDLETON)   (BLACKROCK)

Tim Crowley 0-1   *Pat Horgan 0-1*   *Jimmy Barry-Murphy*
(GLEN ROVERS)   (GLEN ROVERS)   (ST FINBARR'S)

Seánie O'Leary 1-0   *Ray Cummins*   *Eamonn O'Donoghue 1-1*
(BLACKROCK)   (BLACKROCK)   (BLACKROCK)

Subs: Pat Moylan (BLACKROCK) *for McCurtain, Charlie McCarthy* (ST FINBARR'S) *for Cummins. Also Ger Cunningham* (ST FINBARR'S), *Denis Burns* (ST FINBARR'S), *Donal O'Grady* (ST FINBARR'S), *Danny Buckley* (BLACKROCK)

SELECTORS
Frank Murphy, Jimmy Brohan, Denis Murphy, Tim Mullane, Johnny Clifford

REFEREE
Jim Landers
(WATERFORD)

10

1981: Limerick win their seventeenth title

The 1981 Munster senior championship was regarded as one of the most exciting in years, with all the games providing hurling of a very high and entertaining standard. Clare defeated a well-rated Waterford side in the first round, and then went on to defeat the highly rated league champions, Cork, in a thrilling semi-final at Thurles. Limerick came back from the dead in their semi-final meeting with Tipperary at Thurles, and then won the replay in the Gaelic Grounds. They went on to win the decider with Clare in an absorbing game that saw Joe McKenna score three goals.

Clare and Waterford met at Thurles on 24 May. Waterford went into the game as favourites as a result of their display in the league, in which they were beaten by

Cork, the eventual winners, in the semi-final, a game in which they were well in contention until the last five minutes. They had also beaten Clare in the quarter-final. Clare, on the other hand, hadn't got back to the heights of 1978. A number of new players had been introduced from the successful St Flannan's teams of 1976 and 79, Barry Smythe, Leo McQuillan, Martin Meehan and Gerry McInerney.

Clare were without Jim Power and Pat O'Connor, and had to start without Seán Hehir who cried off with a hamstring injury. The game was very even during the first twenty minutes, with the sides level on four occasions, but Waterford got the upper hand in the final ten minutes and went into the break leading 0-7 to 0-5. It might have been greater had Noel Connors reacted more quickly to a loose ball at the edge of the Clare goalmouth just before the break.

Clare made a better start to the second half and were level within ten minutes. A couple of minutes later they had the first of their three goals. Johnny Callinan made the opening for Noel Ryan to score. However, Waterford came back with a goal by Jim Green, after winning the ball from a long clearance by Liam O'Brien. This left the score 1-11 to 1-9 in Clare's favour, but they added to their advantage in the fifty-seventh minute when Leo Quinlan got their second goal.

Instead of Clare capitalising on their advantage, it was Waterford who began to play with more determination, scoring four points without reply to leave a single point between the sides. The game was still wide open. Clare came back with a point, but then

Waterford went ahead with a second goal from Stephen Breen to go in front with only three minutes remaining.

Clare's reply was swift and decisive. Declan Coote struck a powerful goal after a pass from Gerry McInerney. Waterford had nothing in reserve and Clare had the last say with a McInerney point to give them victory by 3-14 to 2-14.

———

Limerick and Tipperary played in the semi-final at Thurles on 7 June. This was an amazing game with Tipperary thirteen points in front on a scoreline of 2-10 to 0-3, and apparently set for victory at half-time. They seemed a transformed side from that which exited the league at the quarter-final stage against Laois when they lost a nine-point half-time lead. When John Grogan, who made a return to the Tipperary side that day after a three-year absence, added a point on the resumption, any doubts in the minds of their supporters of a repeat of the Nowlan Park calamity were calmed.

However, the game changed in a dramatic and sudden manner. Limerick began to assert themselves at centre field and Brian Carroll — his brother Mossie made his debut at centre back for Tipperary the same day — unsettled Tipperary with a long-range goal in the sixth minute. Then disaster really struck in an eight-minute spell between the sixteenth and twenty-fourth minutes when Joe McKenna crashed home three goals to put Limerick in front. Tipperary came back to go ahead with a Pat Fox point, but McKenna climaxed a great personal performance with an equalising point two minutes from time.

The replay was at Limerick two weeks later and Tipperary were beaten comprehensively 3-17 to 2-12. They showed neither the grit, the guts nor the ability to lower the colours of the reigning champions. With a slight breeze in their favour in the first half, Tipperary gave a subdued performance and Limerick were well in control by 2-8 to 0-6 at the interval. Tipperary gave their supporters some hope in the third quarter, but they flattered only to deceive and Limerick fully deserved their eight-point advantage at the final whistle.

The team showed a number of changes from the drawn game. Leonard Enright came on in place of Donal Murray at full back, Mick Grimes in place of Jimmy Carroll at centre field, Paddy Kelly in place of Ger Mulcahy at wing forward, and Willie Fitzmaurice for David O'Riordan at corner forward.

LIMERICK

Tommy Quaid

Paudie Fitzmaurice (CAPT.)   *Leonard Enright*   *Pat Herbert*

Liam O'Donoghue   *Seán Foley*   *Dom Punch*

Brian Carroll   *Mick Grimes*

Ollie O'Connor   *John Flanagan*   *Paddy Kelly*

Willie Fitzmaurice   *Joe McKenna*   *Eamon Cregan*

Sub: Frankie Nolan for Herbert

Clare created a major shock when they defeated a strongly fancied Cork in the second semi-final at Thurles on 14 June. Clare gave an outstanding performance to gain their first championship victory over the opposition in twenty-six years. The success was hewn from outstanding performances by the long-standing members of the team, particularly the half-back line of Ger Loughnane, Seán Stack and Seán Hehir, and Johnny Callinan and Enda O'Connor up front. Cork had to line out without flu victim Ray Cummins.

The game was even in the opening quarter with the sides level on three occasions. When Jimmy Barry-Murphy goaled in the fourteenth minute, he put Cork ahead by 1-4 to 0-3. Matters remained fairly even with both sides exchanging points until the thirtieth minute when Enda O'Connor goaled for Clare and put them into the lead, 1-8 to 1-7. Cork came back with a great point by John Fenton to level, and just before the half-time whistle Clare were unlucky not to get a second goal.

The sides exchanged points in the opening minutes after the resumption and then Clare got a tremendous psychological boost when Leo Quinlan put them into the lead with an opportunist goal. A powerful shot by Johnny Callinan was blocked by Ger Cunningham in the Cork goal, and Quinlan finished it to the net. This score was to sustain Clare when Cork came with a strong challenge later in the half. Another blow for Clare was struck in the fifty-first minute when Séamus Durack stopped a penalty by Pat Horgan. Clare were also helped by the inaccuracy of the Cork forwards who had ten wides in the second half.

However, Cork remained very much in the game, and when John Horgan pointed a 70 soon after failing with the penalty, Cork were only a point in arrears, 2-10 to 1-12. But Clare went further in front with points by Noel Ryan, Gerry McInerney and two by Tony Nugent, and with five minutes remaining were five points to the good. At this stage Cork's chances were revived with a goal by Tim Crowley, but Clare came back with a Martin Meehan point to leave a goal between the sides. They should have scored a goal soon after, but Noel Ryan failed with the chance. With less than two minutes remaining, Jimmy Barry-Murphy got possession about forty yards out and elected to hit it instead of coming closer. It screamed over the bar, and with it went Cork's chance of a draw. It would have been a cruel blow for Clare had he scored a goal, and they survived by 2-15 to 2-13 for a memorable victory.

CLARE

Séamus Durack (CAPT.)

Barry Smythe	*John Ryan*	*Tommy Keane*
Ger Loughnane	*Seán Stack*	*Seán Hehir*
	Declan Coote	*Tony Nugent*
Johnny Callinan	*Enda O'Connor*	*Martin Meehan*
Leo Quinlan	*Noel Ryan*	*Gerry McInerney*

The pairing of Limerick and Clare in the Munster final at Thurles on 5 July was an exciting one. They were traditional rivals who always gave of their best when drawn against one another. Many of the players had been rivals at school level also, having faced one another in the Harty Cup. On this occasion Limerick were champions and seeking to retain their title. The two games against Tipperary had given them an opportunity to discover their best fifteen, as well as a psychological boost.

Clare had reason to be confident about their prospects. They had built on a promising performance against Waterford by beating league champions and favourites, Cork, in the semi-final. Their team was a blend of the old and the tried as well as the new and the enthusiastic. Tony Nugent and Declan Coote were playing outstanding hurling at centre field.

In the end it was the brilliance of Joe McKenna that dashed Clare's hopes. The game was delicately balanced until ten minutes from the end, when the Limerick full forward hit his third all-important goal, which wiped out the element of uncertainty and paved the way for a comfortable six-point victory.

The game attracted just over 40,000 spectators and was played in ideal conditions. In the first half, which was largely dominated by Clare, the marking was so close that the hurling lacked any real fluency. Clare had wind advantage and were fortunate when referee George Ryan of Tipperary disallowed a McKenna goal in the third minute, apparently because the full forward was inside the square when he took the pass from

Paddy Kelly. Midfielder Declan Coote had the first score a minute later, and after McKenna succeeded in goaling in the sixth minute, Clare showed great confidence and maturity by cancelling out the score immediately afterwards. From a puck-out Martin Meehan shot down the left flank and full forward Noel Ryan, under pressure from Leonard Enright, did well to goal from an awkward angle.

This score boosted Clare and as the game progressed they looked more dangerous in attack. In contrast, the Limerick forward line was well held, particularly in the full line where McKenna and Cregan were given few openings.

Limerick failed to take advantage of a penalty awarded to McKenna in the twentieth minute, Cregan hitting the ball weakly along the ground, but McKenna got a point when the clearance came to him. This put the sides level at 1-2 each, but after Clare went back in front with a Callinan point, they scored a second goal in the twenty-second minute from a well-hit penalty by Gerry McInerney.

At this stage Limerick came back into the reckoning with three points, one from a Cregan free, and two from play from Jimmy Carroll. This left Limerick only a point in arrears with ten minutes to the interval. However, it was Clare who came back with two points during this period, the result of the dominance of Seán Stack at centre back. They might also have had two further goals, a good shot from John Ryan being stopped by Leonard Enright's thigh, and a penalty by McInerney driven wide. At the half-time whistle Clare were leading

2-5 to 1-5, and although the margin was small, with the wind in their favour their overall form promised well for the second half.

It was Limerick who made significant progress on the resumption. With Liam O'Donoghue outstanding, they scored four points in the first five minutes to only one reply from Clare to put the sides level at 2-6 to 1-9. Limerick were set to go in front in the forty-first minute until Cregan missed a free. Instead, Colm Honan, who was introduced, pointed for Clare.

Limerick came more into the game at this stage, chiefly through the growing dominance of Mick Grimes and Jimmy Carroll in the centre of the field, as well as the continued fine display by Seán Foley at centre back, but the forwards made little headway until Joe McKenna received a pass from substitute, Willie Fitzmaurice, and managed to finish the ball to the Clare net.

Limerick missed a number of chances and Leo Quinlan kept Clare in contention with a point. They were further helped with an equalising point in the fifty-seventh minute by Tony Nugent, who was now operating at centre forward, with Pat O'Connor gone to centre field to try to shore up their effort in that area.

The turning point in the game came in the sixtieth minute when McKenna had his third goal following a clearance from Quaid. Willie Fitzmaurice crossed from the left, McKenna lifted the ball and, tackled by Ryan, turned and hand-passed it over the head of Séamus Durack into the Clare goal.

Fitzmaurice added an insurance point four minutes later and victory was secured before Cregan pointed two late frees to give Limerick a six-point victory on a scoreline of 3-12 to 2-9. McKenna finished with a total of 3-3 which, added to his 4-3 in the two games with Tipperary, revealed how influential and important he was to Limerick's success. Victory gave Limerick their seventeenth title and their first in successive years since 1974, when they met Clare previously in the final.

LIMERICK

Tommy Quaid
(FEOHANAGH)

Paudie Fitzmaurice	*Leonard Enright*	*Pat Herbert*
(KILLEEDY, CAPT.)	(PATRICKSWELL)	(AHANE)

Liam O'Donoghue 0-1	*Seán Foley*	*Dom Punch*
(MUNGRET)	(PATRICKSWELL)	(PATRICKSWELL)

Mike Grimes   *Jimmy Carroll 0-1*
(SOUTH LIBERTIES) (HOSPITAL-HERBERTSTOWN)

Paddy Kelly	*John Flanagan 0-2*	*Brian Carroll*
(KILMALLOCK)	(FEOHANAGH)	(GARRYSPILLANE)

Ollie O'Connor	*Joe McKenna 3-3*	*Eamon Cregan 0-4*
(BALLYBROWN)	(SOUTH LIBERTIES)	(CLAUGHAUN)

Sub: Willie Fitzmaurice (KILLEEDY) *0-1 for Kelly. Also Séamus O'Sullivan* (TOURNAFULLA), *John McCarthy* (KILFINANE), *Connie Keating* (MUNGRET), *Ger Mulcahy* (DROMIN-ATHLACCA), *Ger McMahon* (ST PATRICK'S), *Davy O'Riordan* (KILMALLOCK), *Timmy Burke* (DROMCOLLOGHER), *Frankie Nolan* (PATRICKSWELL), *Pat Foley* (PATRICKSWELL)

SELECTORS

Noel Drumgoole, J. P. Ryan, Vincent Byrnes, Timmy Horgan

CLARE

Séamus Durack
(ÉIRE ÓG, CAPT.)

Barry Smythe
(BANNER)

John Ryan
(NEWMARKET ON FERGUS)

Tom Keane
(KILMALEY)

Ger Loughnane
(FEAKLE)

Seán Stack
(SIXMILEBRIDGE)

Seán Hehir
(O'CALLAGHAN'S MILLS)

Tony Nugent 0-1
(ÉIRE ÓG)

Declan Coote 0-2
(ÉIRE ÓG)

Johnny Callinan 0-2
(CLARECASTLE)

Enda O'Connor 0-1
(TUBBER)

Martin Meehan
(KILMALEY)

Leo Quinlan 0-1
(SIXMILEBRIDGE)

Noel Ryan 1-0
(ÉIRE ÓG)

Gerry McInerney 1-0
(SIXMILEBRIDGE)

Subs: Pat O'Connor (TUBBER) *0-1 for Meehan, Colm Honan* (CLONLARA) *0-1 for McInerney, Martin Nugent* (ÉIRE ÓG) *for Eamon O'Connor. Also Jim Power* (TULLA), *Michael O'Connor* (BRUFF), *Johnny McMahon* (NEWMARKET), *Seán Heaslip* (ÉIRE ÓG), *Pat Morey* (SIXMILEBRIDGE), *Colm Mahon* (ÉIRE ÓG), *Mike Deasy* (O'CALLAGHAN'S MILLS), *Seán McMahon* (NEWMARKET), *Jimmy Walsh* (BODYKE)

REFEREE

George Ryan
(TIPPERARY)

11

1984: The Centenary Munster final

The Centenary Year of the GAA was a very special one. It was a time to look back on a century of achievement and take pride in belonging to one of the greatest amateur associations in the world. It was a time also to review progress in the promotion of Irish games and pastimes and make plans for the future.

More particularly it was to bring a new intensity to the hurling championship as counties looked upon winning the centenary title as something especially desirable. There was to be a new focus on training and preparation. This was to be of particular importance in Tipperary, where the association was founded in 1884 and where the county was often referred to as 'the home of the GAA'. Also, the county had been in the hurling doldrums for so long, with no Munster final victory since 1971, and a gap of ten years before recording their first championship victory in 1983. Their supporters hoped that the county might take its place once more among the greats in hurling. A special incentive would be to stop Cork winning three in a row.

Munster teams did well in the two senior hurling competitions that preceded the championship. Limerick won the league, defeating Wexford comprehensively in the final 3-16 to 1-9. The winners had accounted for Tipperary, who came through from Division 2, in the semi-final, while Wexford had overcome Cork.

The second competition was the Centenary Cup, an open draw competition that attracted eighteen teams and was played between the league and the championship. Cork and Laois contested the final, with the former winning easily 2-21 to 1-9. Laois had accounted for Tipperary in the quarter-final.

Clare and Waterford met in the first round of the Munster championship at Thurles on 27 May. Neither team had done very well in the league or the Centenary Cup, and the attendance of 5,220 was indicative of the low expectations of the sides. Clare won a dull game 0-15 to 2-8, having conceded a goal in injury time. While Clare deserved to win, Waterford missed two chances for goals in the closing quarter. Clare led 0-8 to 1-4 at half-time, the Waterford goal coming in the fourth minute from Eddie Rockett.

The first of the semi-finals had Cork and Limerick in opposition in the Gaelic Grounds on 3 June. Limerick were superb in the opening quarter, with 1-3 on the scoreboard after seven minutes. Ned Rea scored the goal after Joe McKenna's shot had been saved by Ger Cunningham. Cork did not score until the twelfth minute. They were struggling in a big way at this stage with their unsettled defence, compounded by the advantage Limerick were gaining by controlling centre field, and in the half-back line where Liam O'Donoghue was particularly prominent.

Although winning the toss, Cork elected to play against the breeze and may have been regretting the decision at this stage. However, the trend of the game began to change during the second quarter. Dermot McCurtain began to lift the siege for Cork with an outstanding display at left half-back. Tom Cashman began to come to terms with Paddy Kelly, and Donal O'Grady was dealing better with the threat from Joe McKenna. Side by side with the improved Cork performance was a gradual slowing down of the Limerick attacking machine. As well, there were a number of what turned out to be costly misses from their forward line.

Cork, despite weakness in the forward line, did keep in touch with the odd score, and when Seánie O'Leary goaled in the twenty-eighth minute after Fenton had a twenty-one yard free blocked, they were back in the game with a bang. Limerick threatened again, but they lost chances approaching the break when the score stood at 1-10 to 1-5 in their favour.

The second half was only four minutes old when Paudie Fitzmaurice made a vital interception for Limerick, as Jimmy Barry-Murphy ran in to grab a well-struck pass from Hennessy, only to see the ball swept off his hurley when he was about to strike. But in another four minutes the teams were level when Fenton hit a sideline ball from the left which was touched into the net by Seánie O'Leary after Tommy Quaid had stopped it. O'Leary pointed soon afterwards and the growing Cork confidence was reflected in three more points in the next two minutes from Walsh, Tim Crowley and Hennessy. At this stage Cork were dominant in many areas of the field.

Limerick, who had begun to struggle in attack, moved Brian Carroll to centre forward and he made the opening for McKenna's goal in the forty-eighth minute which brought the sides level. Just before that, Paddy Kelly had Limerick's first score of the half.

Exchanges were hard at this stage with no holes barred and there was great commitment from both sides. McKenna pointed to put Limerick back in front, but almost immediately Fenton scored from play to leave the teams level again at 2-12 each with just over fifteen minutes to go.

Cork made a number of positional changes, and then came the mistake by Quaid which allowed a Fenton sideline shot to go all the way to the net. It was a decisive score from which Limerick never recovered. On the other hand Cork, sensing victory, went on to get three more points, a Fenton free and two from Barry-Murphy. Limerick continued to battle on, a great shot by Flanagan hitting the side of the net with six minutes remaining. Cork had five points to spare on a scoreline of 3-15 to 2-13 at the final whistle.

CORK

Ger Cunningham

Denis Mulcahy   *Donal O'Grady*   *John Hodgins*

Tom Cashman   *John Crowley*   *Dermot McCurtain*

John Fenton (CAPT.)   *Pat Hartnett*

Denis Walsh   *Tim Crowley*   *Kevin Hennessy*

Tomás Mulcahy *Jimmy Barry-Murphy* *Seánie O'Leary*

Sub: John Buckley for Cashman

The second semi-final between Clare and Tipperary was played two weeks later at Thurles. Tipperary supporters went to the game expecting to win, but they got the shock of their lives when it took a Liam Maher snap goal from the rebound of a Séamus Power penalty to give Tipperary a one-point victory in the last minute of the game.

Tipperary were outstanding during the opening twenty minutes, but were made to look very ordinary during the second half. While they could do no wrong during the opening period, Clare struggled to find their rhythm. The home side controlled midfield, penetrated through the centre where Donie O'Connell was beating an uninspiring Seán Stack, and Clare were very much stretched on the wings, particularly on the right where Declan Coote was powerless to limit the threat from Nicky English.

The change in the direction of the game came after twenty minutes, with Tipperary leading 0-7 to 0-1, when their impeccable shooting began to let them down and easy chances were lost. Combined with the brilliance of Declan Corry in the Clare goal, it meant that Tipperary did not get anything like the scores they might have, considering the dominance they enjoyed. The half-time tally showed a mere six points in Tipperary's favour, 0-9 to 0-3, following twelve wides.

The game was transformed soon after the interval when Colm Honan pointed and Gerry McInerney goaled to leave only two points between the sides. Soon after, Sheedy saved a powerful shot from Enda O'Connor. Clare were now playing much better and had gained control over a number of parts of the field. But chances were lost before Tipperary renewed their scoring with a free from Séamus Power in the forty-third minute and three more points in the next five minutes to restore their half-time lead.

Clare were not finished yet and their spirited play saw them pick off some good points. At the other end their back line was making it more difficult for the Tipperary forwards to get through for scores. With ten minutes remaining, the margin between the sides was reduced to a point, before English helped to rally Tipperary with a vital point. Then came a Clare penalty, awarded after substitute Kieran McNamara was fouled, which Gerry McInerney crashed to the net. This was followed by a Callinan point to put Clare in the ascendant.

However, just when it appeared that Clare had done enough to win, a Tipperary attack initiated by substitute Michael Doyle led to English being pulled down when he was in a threatening position. The save from the resulting penalty by Séamus Power was finished to the net by Liam Maher to give Tipperary the slimmest of victories, 1-15 to 2-11.

TIPPERARY

John Sheedy

Jack Bergin	*Jim Keogh*	*Dinny Cahill*
Pat Fitzell	*John McIntyre*	*Bobby Ryan* (CAPT.)
	Ralph O'Callaghan	*Philip Kennedy*
Nicky English	*Donie O'Connell*	*Liam Maher*
Tom Waters	*Séamus Power*	*Noel O'Dwyer*

Subs: Michael Doyle for Waters, Gerry Stapleton for McIntyre

The stage was set for what was to be an epic encounter between Cork and Tipperary at Thurles on 15 July. In the aftermath it was to be called the 'best-ever' Munster final, and it did have an intensity which set it apart from other more mundane encounters between the sides. The final minutes will be frozen for ever in the minds of the 50,000-odd spectators who witnessed it as Cork conjured up a fairytale finish, highlighted by Seánie O'Leary's match-winning goal, which left Tipperary shattered and demoralised. It was a fitting classic for Centenary Year.

Going into the game Cork were undoubted favourites, having easily won the previous two finals against disappointing Waterford sides. Tipperary had done nothing to raise expectations after their many years in the wilderness, apart from a traditional ability to lift their performance against Cork. Realistically, they had won their first championship game in ten years the previous season and their performances in the league, the Centenary Cup and their semi-final encounter with Clare hadn't revealed any dramatic improvement in the side.

But all this was quickly forgotten after Tipperary went into the lead fifteen minutes into the second half and proceeded to outhurl the Cork side, which had looked marginally superior at the interval. With John McIntyre the main inspirational force at centre back, Tipperary were able to assume almost total control as Cork struggled to find a rhythm in attack. Jimmy Barry-Murphy missed an open goal nine minutes from the end, and in another two minutes Tipperary were four points in front and seemingly heading for victory. This was a moment of ecstasy for the Tipperary supporters as they looked forward to the spoils of victory. But it soon changed to the agony of defeat as Cork scored 2-2 in the final minutes to snatch a sensational victory. The disappointment for Tipperary was all the greater as victory had come so tantalisingly close. To say it was a great Tipperary effort from a very gutsy team was no consolation for a county starved of success in the senior ranks. In the situation a near miss was as shattering as a massive defeat.

Cork made one change from the side that defeated Limerick in the semi-final. Pat Horgan came on at wing forward in place of Denis Walsh. As it transpired, the latter replaced Horgan in the sixty-second minute of the game. Tipperary also had one change from their semi-final side, with Michael Doyle coming on at right corner forward in place of Tom Waters.

In the aftermath of defeat, Tipperary's effort was revealed as dogged by misfortune and some doubtful selection decisions. The decision to play Pat Fitzell was the wrong one as he carried an injury into the game; too much damage was done before he was replaced after twenty-eight minutes. Unfortunate too was Dinny Cahill's muscle trouble which forced his retirement after only twelve minutes. Another misfortune was Bobby Ryan's injury and departure after forty-five minutes, as he was playing a stormer. To many the most incomprehensible decision was to bring Séamus Power back into the defence from his full forward position, where he was having a fine game and giving the Cork full back so many problems that he was replaced.

Kevin Hennessy opened the scoring for Cork after five minutes, but Tipperary received a real boost with an opportunist goal from Séamus Power less than a minute later. The balance of power shifted very much towards Cork when Barry-Murphy had two good goals in the space of five minutes to give his side the lead by five points. Donie O'Connell brought Tipperary back into contention with a twenty-third minute goal, but Cork soon opened up a five-point lead again. Just before half-time English, who had moved to corner forward, gave Tipperary a major boost with a goal to leave the half-time score 2-10 to 3-5 in Cork's favour.

The second half was only two minutes old when Tipperary almost got another goal, but Power's effort hit the side netting. A few minutes later the same player pointed a free, and in the fortieth minute Cork replied with a Hennessy point. They were to score only one further point between then and five minutes from the end.

At this stage Cork were unable to match their first-half performance, lacking cohesion in their defence and penetration in the forwards. Numerous changes and switches were made. Pat Horgan was moved to centre forward to try to curtail McIntyre, while Tim Crowley was replaced by Tony O'Sullivan. Earlier, John Blake came in to replace Donal O'Grady at full back.

Substitute Paul Dooley equalised for Tipperary in the forty-eighth minute, and a minute later Maher put them ahead. With the crowd rising to them, Tipperary began to hurl with a confidence and self-assurance which belied their lack of experience. Hartnett brought Cork level once again, but it was Tipperary who continued to force the pace. They got a penalty with fifteen minutes remaining, and Power pointed Tipperary back in front. O'Dwyer pointed a free in the sixtieth minute, and Cork missed a great opportunity for a goal when Barry-Murphy shot wide.

Cork were still in contention, but when Kennedy pointed a 70 and O'Dwyer sent over another free to give Tipperary a four-point lead with seven minutes remaining, it looked ominous for Cork. It remained so until a Fenton point from a free was followed by an equalising goal from Tony O'Sullivan, who finished the ball to the net after goalkeeper John Sheedy brought off a fine save from Hartnett. Fenton then had two wides before the game was saved by Cork.

It began when Mulcahy made a crucial interception after Michael Doyle crossed from the left corner. O'Sullivan collected the clearance and tried for a point. After Sheedy appeared to stop the ball from going over the bar, it was quickly smashed to the net by the vigilant O'Leary. Fenton's late point brought Tipperary's titanic struggle to an inglorious end, but even in defeat the richness of their hurling and the assurance of their play earned them a pride which had been lacking for some time.

In the post-mortems that inevitably followed the result, there were two great 'ifs': what if Doyle's pass had reached English? What would have happened had Sheedy not stopped the ball going over the bar? However, such speculation hadn't the slightest bearing on the result, which showed Cork the winners by 4-15 to 3-14.

CORK

Ger Cunningham
(St Finbarr's)

Denis Mulcahy   *Donal O'Grady*   *John Hodgins*
(Midleton)   (St Finbarr's)   (St Finbarr's)

Tom Cashman   *John Crowley*   *Dermot McCurtain*
(Blackrock)   (Bishopstown)   (Blackrock)

John Fenton 0-7   *Pat Hartnett 0-1*
(Midleton, capt.)   (Midleton)

Pat Horgan 0-3   *Tim Crowley*   *Kevin Hennessy 0-3*
(Glen Rovers)   (Newcestown)   (Midleton)

Tomás Mulcahy   *Jimmy Barry-Murphy 2-0*   *Seánie O'Leary 1-1*
(Glen Rovers)   (St Finbarr's)   (Youghal)

Subs: John Blake (St Finbarr's) *for O'Grady, Tony O'Sullivan* (Na Piarsaigh) *1-0 for Crowley, Denis Walsh* (Cloughduv) *for Horgan. Also Ger Power* (Midleton), *John Buckley* (Glen Rovers), *John Hartnett (Midleton)*

SELECTORS

Joe Desmond, Denis Hurley, Fr Michael O'Brien, Justin McCarthy, Tom Monaghan, Noel Collins

TIPPERARY
John Sheedy
(Portroe)

Jack Bergin   *Jim Keogh*   *Dinny Cahill*
(Moycarkey-Borris)   (Silvermines)   (Kilruane-MacDonaghs)

Pat Fitzell   *John McIntyre*   *Bobby Ryan*
(Cashel King Cormac's)   (Lorrha)   (Borrisoleigh, capt.)

Ralph O'Callaghan   *Philip Kennedy 0-2*
(Carrick Davins)   (Éire Óg, Nenagh)

Nicky English 1-0   *Donie O'Connell 1-2*   *Liam Maher 0-1*
(Lattin-Cullen)   (Killenaule)   (Boherlahan-Dualla)

Michael Doyle   *Séamus Power 1-6*   *Noel O'Dwyer 0-2*
(Holycross-Ballycahill)   (Boherlahan-Dualla)   (Borrisoleigh)

Subs: John Doyle (Holycross-Ballycahill) *for Cahill, Brian Heffernan* (Éire Óg, Nenagh) *for Fitzell, Paul Dooley* (Borrisokane) *0-1 for Ryan. Also John Farrell* (Kickhams), *Tom Waters* (Carrick Swan), *Austin Buckley* (Cappawhite), *Gerry Stapleton* (Borrisoleigh), *Pat McGrath* (Loughmore-Castleiney), *John Grace* (Silvermines), *Mick Ryan* (Borrisoleigh)

SELECTORS
Pat Stakelum, Liam Hennessy, Fr Ray Reidy, Len Gaynor, John Kelly

REFEREE
John Moore
(Waterford)

12

1987: Tipperary end the famine

The 1987 Munster final was memorable in many ways. It completed a championship that had seen four draws, two in the semi-finals and the final twice. It brought in huge money to the coffers of the Munster Council. It saw the end of a famine in senior hurling victories for Tipperary, a lack of success that stretched back to 1971. In contrast, it saw the end of Cork's quest for six-in-a-row final victories.

The 1987 Munster championship was a bonanza year for the Munster Council. It took eight matches instead of the usual five to complete the championship. As a result of three match replays, two semi-finals and a final, the council earned unprecedented gate receipts of £1,336,036, a massive increase of £837,947 on the previous year's figure. In addition, the council gained from its policy of booking stand seating and the pre-sale of stand tickets prior to major games. There were no fewer than six ticket games and £698,407 of the total gate receipts came from the pre-sale of stand tickets.

There wasn't much inkling of the excitement ahead when the two first round games were played on 24 May. Although Limerick won by 2-15 to 1-14 at Thurles, it was Waterford who gave the more distinguished performance. In a scrappy and uninspiring game, Waterford kept their heads in front until seventeen minutes from time, when Danny Fitzgerald's goal revived Limerick and sent them on to victory. The winners, who lined out without Leonard Enright, were shaky in defence and attack, lacked leadership and, most of all, scoring power.

In the second game, played at Killarney, Tipperary looked very ordinary at times against lowly rated Kerry. Although they won in the end by 1-21 to 2-6, their victory did not come with the ease that the scoreline would suggest. Pat Fox was their outstanding forward with a tally of 1-10 to his credit.

Killarney, which got more hurling games than normal in 1987, was the venue for the Clare-Tipperary clash in the Munster semi-final on 7 June. Tipperary made a number of changes. John Kennedy was centre back in place of Noel Sheehy, with Paul Delaney coming in on the wing. Philip Kennedy was replaced at centre field by John McGrath. In a reshuffled forward line Jerry Williams, Bobby Ryan and Nicky English came in for Michael Scully, Michael Doyle and Liam Stokes.

The game was even in the first half, at the end of which Clare, who had played with the breeze, held the advantage 0-8 to 1-4. It remained tight in the third quarter with the sides level on four occasions. During this period Clare were reduced to fourteen men following the dismissal of full forward Tommy Guilfoyle. Tipperary gradually pulled in front and were four points to the good with eight minutes remaining. But poor finishing lost them their advantage. Instead, Cyril Lyons reduced the margin to three points and, with inspired defending by the Clare backs led by Seán Stack, Tipperary were prevented from scoring during the final minutes. Then, one minute into injury time, Gerry McInerney collected a cross from Alan Cunningham and sent a powerful shot all the way to the Tipperary net for a dramatic equaliser on a scoreline of 1-13 each.

The replay at the same venue two weeks later was a much different affair. Tipperary brought in John Heffernan at corner back in place of Peter Brennan, and Joe Hayes was on in place of John McGrath at centre field. In one of the most one-sided Munster senior hurling championship games in years, Tipperary defeated Clare by 4-17 to 0-8. The replay was as good as over at the interval, by which time Tipperary had raced to a 2-9 to 0-4 lead, despite having played against the breeze. Four minutes after resuming, Donie O'Connell scored Tipperary's third goal, and after that there was no way back for Clare. Nicky English was the highest scorer for the winners with 2-4

The second semi-final, between Cork and Limerick at Thurles on 14 June, also ended in a draw, 3-11 each. It took a Cork point in injury time to secure the draw in a highly exciting game. Inspired by Tommy Quaid's brilliant goalkeeping, Limerick rallied magnificently to wipe out a seven-point deficit and take the lead with Shane Fitzgibbon's dramatic goal three minutes from time. Then Cork missed three chances before Kevin Kingston rescued them with a last-gasp equalising point.

It was a remarkable climax to a game which went very much Limerick's way in the early stages, swung in Cork's direction after the switch of Teddy McCarthy to midfield, and stayed within their grasp after Kingston goaled thirteen minutes into the second half. It looked all over as Cork controlled the play, although they failed to utilise all their scoring chances. The direction of the game changed after the second Limerick goal from Gary Kirby in the sixty-first minute. The scene was then set for the dramatic finish. Cork led by the minimum, 1-7 to 1-6, at the interval.

As in the replay in the Tipperary-Clare semi-final, Cork made no mistake in the replay at Thurles two weeks later. In a vintage display they never gave Limerick a look-in and won 3-14 to 0-10. Cork reshuffled their team for the replay and brought in John Crowley in place of Tom Cashman in the backs and John Fitzgibbon for Gerry Fitzgerald in the forwards. The winners, on song from the opening exchanges, were inspired by a brilliant goal from John Fenton, who doubled on a ball from about forty yards out and sent it all the way to the net with awesome velocity just before half-time, and led 3-7 to 0-6 at the interval. There was no resurrection for Limerick on the resumption. All they could manage were four isolated points, and the exodus from Semple Stadium had begun long before the final whistle sounded.

——⋙——

The Munster final at Thurles on 12 July will be remembered as the 'Great Escape' game! In fact there were two escapes. Tipperary were leading by seven points with less than twenty minutes remaining, and apparently coasting along. But Cork came back with a magnificent recovery from John Fenton's impressive scoring contribution, and were ahead with time up. It took an equalising point from a free by Pat Fox in injury time to rescue Tipperary from the jaws of defeat and send the sides to a replay on a scoreline of 1-18 each.

Cork fielded the same lineout as against Limerick in the replay. Tipperary made one change from their semi-final side, John McGrath coming in at wing forward in place of Jerry Williams. The expectation of the game was reflected in the huge crowd: over 56,000 attended, with another uncounted 5,000 children in the ground. Tipperary opened well and were four points to two in front at the end of the first quarter. Cork missed a couple of goal opportunities and experienced major problems in the attack during this opening period. At the other end Tipperary were piling pressure on the Cork backs, and they were doing well at centre field, where Joe Hayes had a great game until he burned himself out in the second half. The Tipperary half-forward line were also doing well, while the full forward line made little headway against Cork's inner defence.

Although Tipperary held the advantage, they were not putting away as many scores as their control of the game would suggest. On the other hand Cork, although their forwards were failing to score, were keeping in touch through John Fenton's impeccable free-taking. Ten points out of his total of twelve in the game were to come from placed balls. Cork made a few changes, but they failed to improve matters and they trailed 0-11 to 0-7 at the interval, with Fenton responsible for five of Cork's points.

Cork opened the second half with a couple of good goal chances, one of them from Kevin Kingston, foiled by a great save from Ken Hogan. Tony O'Sullivan came more into the game and made the most of any chances that came his way. Another good goal opportunity by Fitzgibbon was also saved by Hogan.

The Tipperary selectors began to reshuffle their forwards after the team had gone ten minutes without a score, and English was switched to full forward. It was to prove a lucky move when in the forty-ninth minute he got behind the defence without his hurley and had the composure to hesitate before kicking the ball past Cunningham. It left Tipperary leading by 1-14 to 0-10 and seemingly in a strong position.

But Cork came thundering back into the game, with improved performances in many areas plus four vital points. The introduction of Michael Mullins for Tomás Mulcahy had put new life into the half-forward line.

Kingston came more into the game and O'Sullivan continued to impress. Jim Cashman steadied matters in the back line when he moved back after Dermot McCurtain was replaced.

Cork's revival had the deficit down to two points with ten minutes remaining and Tipperary realised they were in trouble. At this critical stage they missed vital scoring opportunities from play and from frees. Fox broke the deadlock when he scored a point in the sixty-fifth minute to leave a goal between the sides.

However, this failed to halt Cork's momentum. Fenton pointed a free a minute later, and then came the Cork goal. Hennessy got possession and played the ball to Mullins. He missed it, but Kingston made no mistake with a powerful ground shot. This put Cork into a sensational lead. With less than three minutes remaining, Fenton had another point. Fox reduced it to a point with a fifty yard free and it seemed as if Cork had won as injury time arrived. However, in the final minute Fox squeezed over the equalising point to leave the sides level at 1-18 each. It was a remarkable climax to a game which for so long promised to go Tipperary's way and which, in the final analysis, was almost Cork's for the taking.

CORK

Ger Cunningham

Denis Mulcahy   *Richard Browne*   *John Crowley*

Dermot McCurtain   *Pat Hartnett*   *Denis Walsh*

John Fenton 0-12   *Jim Cashman*

Teddy McCarthy 0-1 Tomás Mulcahy   Tony O'Sullivan 0-4

John Fitzgibbon   Kevin Hennessy (CAPT.) 0-1   Kevin Kingston 1-0

Subs: Michael Mullins for Mulcahy, Pat O'Connor for McCurtain, Gerry Fitzgerald for Fitzgibbon

TIPPERARY
Ken Hogan

John Heffernan   Conor O'Donovan   Séamus Gibson

Richard Stakelum (CAPT.) 0-1   John Kennedy   Paul Delaney

Joe Hayes   Colm Bonnar

John McGrath 0-1   Donie O'Connell 0-4   Aidan Ryan 0-2

Pat Fox 0-9   Bobby Ryan   Nicky English 1-1

Subs: Liam Stokes for McGrath, Philip Kenny for Hayes

REFEREE
Terence Murray
(LIMERICK)

The replay was fixed for Killarney the following Sunday. Both sides wanted a new home and away agreement, but the sticking point was who would have home fixture first. Because Tipperary had travelled to Cork for the first cycle in the previous agreement, they thought Cork should come to Thurles first on this occasion. Another argument in favour of Thurles was that it was the only venue in Munster capable of holding 60,000 spectators, the number expected for the replay. The suggestion was dismissed by Cork and the game went to Killarney.

Apart from the difficulties getting there, and the fact that the Munster Council limited the crowd to 45,000, Killarney had always been a happy hunting ground for Tipperary. And it was to prove so once more. It took extra time to do it, but at the finish Tipperary were nine points ahead on a scoreline of 4-22 to 1-22.

Tipperary made a couple of changes for the replay, Pat Fitzell replacing Joe Hayes at centre field and Jerry Williams coming in for John McGrath at wing forward. Nicky English exchanged places with Bobby Ryan in the full forward line. On the Cork side Jim Cashman replaced Dermot McCurtain at wing back, with Tom Cashman coming in at centre field. Michael Mullins came in at wing forward and Tomás Mulcahy went into the full forward line, displacing John Fitzgibbon.

The eventual outcome did not appear a likely prospect in the opening half as Cork raced to a seven to one point lead, despite playing against the breeze. Tipperary steadied up somewhat as the game progressed and had the lead reduced to 1-10 to 1-5 at the interval. They continued to improve in the second half and by the twenty-third minute had drawn level.

The closing minutes were hectic with Cork edging ahead, and a palmed point by Nicky English required to draw the match, 1-17 each. This came in the dying moments of the game when English gained possession from a long Hogan puck-out. He raced away after winning it. Challenged by two Cork players, he appeared to be tempted to go for a goal but then decided to take the point instead and ensure a draw at least.

The second half produced a number of talking points. Midway through the period a Pat Fox shot rebounded and it wasn't clear whether it came back off an upright or off one of the stanchions in the goal. To balance this, in the sixty-ninth minute a shot from Teddy McCarthy was finished to the net by Tony O'Sullivan for what appeared a perfectly legitimate goal. But, with a speed that was remarkable, the umpires crossed flags to disallow the score without consulting with the referee.

So, extra time had to be played. Cork were to be without the two Cashmans, as Tom had retired during the second half and Jim did not reappear in extra time. John Fenton also carried an injury into the extra period and moved to corner forward. Despite these setbacks Cork opened up a two-point lead early in the first half of extra time and led by 1-21 to 1-20.

By this stage Tipperary had lost Delaney and the selectors moved back Bobby Ryan and introduced Michael Doyle at full forward. Doyle's selection was to pay rich dividends in the second period of extra time. First, Fox levelled from a free and O'Connell pointed after four minutes to put Tipperary in front for the first time in the game. A minute and a half later came the match-winning score when a shot from O'Connell was deflected off Browne, and Doyle calmly ushered it over the line. Three minutes later he scored again after an attempted clearance by Browne was returned by Fitzell. Then after Fenton failed to goal from a twenty-one yard free, Tipperary produced another goal, this time from O'Connell. After that Cork had neither the time nor the capability to even attempt a recovery. Tipperary were completely on top on a scoreline of 4-22 to 1-22.

The scenes of jubilation were immense. All the winning players were acclaimed as heroes. It was heaven to be a Tipperary supporter in Killarney on the day. Captain, Richard Stakelum, led the supporters in the singing of 'Slievenamon', and he introduced his speech with the words, 'The famine is over', which encapsulated the wonderful experience of the occasion and gave expression to the deepest feelings of Tipperary people everywhere. The famine had lasted eighteen years; 1971 was a long way back. Tipperary had won and in doing so had prevented Cork winning six in a row.

The result was all so frustrating for Cork, outstanding in the first half and within seconds of that record six in a row, but then weakened by injuries and ultimately demoralised by Tipperary's whirlwind finish.

It was an occasion to savour for a whole new generation of Tipperary supporters and for those who had begun to forget what winning was all about. It was particularly satisfying for team manager Babs Keating, a member of the last winning team at the same Fitzgerald Stadium, and for co-selectors Theo English and Donie Nealon who had also shared in that distant success.

TIPPERARY

Ken Hogan

(LORRHA)

John Heffernan *Conor O'Donovan* *Séamus Gibson*
(ÉIRE ÓG, NENAGH) (ÉIRE ÓG, NENAGH) (KILRUANE-MACDONAGHS)

Richard Stakelum *John Kennedy* *Paul Delaney 0-2*
(BORRISOLEIGH, CAPT.) (CLONOULTY-ROSSMORE) (ROSCREA)

Colm Bonnar *Pat Fitzell 0-1*
(CASHEL KING CORMAC'S)(CASHEL KING CORMAC'S)

Jerry Williams *Donie O'Connell 1-1* *Aidan Ryan 0-3*
(KILRUANE-MACDONAGHS) (KILLENAULE) (BORRISOLEIGH)

Pat Fox 0-11 *Nicky English 1-1* *Bobby Ryan*
(ÉIRE ÓG, ANACARTY) (LATTIN-CULLEN) (BORRISOLEIGH)

Subs: Martin McGrath (KICKHAMS) 0-3 for Williams, Michael Doyle (HOLYCROSS-BALLYCAHILL) 2-0 for Delaney, Gerry Stapleton (BORRISOLEIGH) for O'Donovan. Also Tony Sheppard (KILRUANE-MACDONAGHS), Philly Kenny (BORRISOLEIGH), Joe Hayes (CLONOULTY-ROSSMORE), Noel Sheehy (SILVERMINES), Liam Stokes (KILSHEELAN), John McGrath (BORRISOLEIGH)

SELECTORS

Michael Babs Keating, Donie Nealon, Theo English

CORK

Ger Cunningham

(ST FINBARR'S)

Denis Mulcahy
(MIDLETON)

Richard Browne
(BLACKROCK)

John Crowley
(BISHOPSTOWN)

Jim Cashman
(BLACKROCK)

Pat Hartnett
(MIDLETON)

Denis Walsh
(ST CATHERINE'S)

John Fenton 0-13
(MIDLETON)

Tom Cashman
(BLACKROCK)

Michael Mullins
(NA PIARSAIGH)

Teddy McCarthy 0-3
(SARSFIELDS)

Tony O'Sullivan 0-3
(NA PIARSAIGH)

Kevin Kingston
(TRACTON)

Kevin Hennessy
(MIDLETON, CAPT.)

Tomás Mulcahy 1-2
(GLEN ROVERS)

Subs: Gerry Fitzgerald (MIDLETON) *0-1 for Mullins, Paul O'Connor* (NA PIARSAIGH) *for Tom Cashman, John Fitzgibbon* (GLEN ROVERS) *for Kingston, Seán O'Gorman* (MILFORD) *for Jim Cashman, Mullins for Fitzgibbon, Dermot McCurtain* (BLACKROCK) *for Crowley. Also Frank O'Sullivan* (GLEN ROVERS), *Seán McCarthy* (BALLINHASSIG)

SELECTORS
Johnny Clifford, Jimmy Brohan, Pat McDonnell, Oliver O'Keeffe, Charlie McCarthy

REFEREE
Terence Murray
(LIMERICK)

13

1990: Cork make hay

Having won the All-Ireland in 1989, beating unlikely finalists Antrim in the process, Tipperary were expected to consolidate their return to the top by winning the 1990 championship. The least that was expected was that they would come through Munster. Instead, they crumbled before a Cork side that produced a splendid performance and played with absolute confidence, shocking Tipperary into a 4-16 to 2-14 defeat. The defeat was reminiscent of a similar day in 1952 when Cork also stopped the Premier county in its quest for four in a row.

Limerick and Clare met in one of the first-round games at Ennis on 13 May. Limerick were favourites going into the game, but the match was so one-sided that they learned little of their true worth from the victory. Clare put up some kind of resistance in the opening twenty minutes before Limerick began to open up a gap, which was six points at the interval, 0-10 to 0-4. It might have been greater but for the lack of cohesion in the Limerick attack. Limerick continued to dominate in the second half and it was a relief to everyone when Willie Barrett blew the final whistle with Limerick in front, 2-16 to 1-5.

The other first-round game between Cork and Kerry at Tralee the following Sunday was expected to be a training session for the visitors, but it didn't turn out quite like that. It was due more to Kerry's shortcomings than Cork's brilliance that victory went to the Corkmen by 3-16 to 3-7. The winners served up a below-par performance and the result might have been different had their opponents been better. With a couple of exceptions, few Cork players enhanced their reputations.

Kerry held their own in the early stages and were only two points in arrears when Cork pounced for two goals. The first of these, scored by Kevin Hennessy in the twenty-first minute, was a real disaster for the Kerry defence which had been holding out manfully up to then. Two minutes later disaster struck again when the Kerry goalkeeper was beaten by a low shot from Brendan O'Sullivan. Kerry came back with a goal from Tony Maunsell, but their joy was short lived before Teddy McCarthy got Cork's third to leave them comfortably in front by 3-6 to 1-5 at the interval. Cork continued to stretch their lead in the third quarter, but then Kerry came back with two opportunist goals that underlined defects in the Cork defence and reduced the deficit to five points with thirteen minutes remaining. But they were unable to make further inroads and Cork had a flurry of late points to win by a margin of nine.

CORK

Ger Cunningham

John Considine   *Seán O'Gorman*   *Denis Walsh*

Kieran McGuckin (CAPT.) *Jim Cashman*   *David Quirke*

Pat Buckley   *Seán McCarthy*

Michael Mullins   *Teddy McCarthy*   *Gerry Fitzgerald*

Kevin Kingston   *Brendan O'Sullivan*   *Kevin Hennessy*

Subs: Mark Foley for Mullins, Tony O'Sullivan for Kingston, Brendan Cunningham for McCarthy

The semi-final pairings brought Cork and Waterford to Thurles on 3 June. It was a much-transformed Cork side that easily overcame a Waterford team which played inexplicably poorly on the day. The previous year, when the two sides met, Cork snatched a fortunate draw before going down by two points in a replay that went to extra time. How Waterford could disimprove so much in twelve months was incomprehensible. In fact Cork were unrated going into the game. However, they produced some powerful defensive play against the wind when it mattered most, and boosted by goals from Kevin Hennessy and Ger Fitzgerald in the fourteenth and twentieth minutes, they assumed a grip which was never afterwards challenged. Waterford failed to score until the fifteenth minute and were behind 2-4 to 0-6 at the interval.

Hennessy struck with Cork's third goal within a minute of the resumption, and when Fitzgerald got their fourth in the fortieth minute, the game was as good as over. A Waterford goal ten minutes later did little to stem the tide as Cork finished with six unanswered points to give them victory by 4-15 to 1-8, and a warning to all and sundry that they were well and truly back.

CORK

Ger Cunningham

John Considine	*Denis Walsh*	*Damien Irwin*
Seán McCarthy	*Jim Cashman*	*Kieran McGuckin* (CAPT.)
	Pat Buckley *Teddy McCarthy*	
Tony O'Sullivan	*Brendan O'Sullivan*	*David Quirke*
Gerry Fitzgerald	*Kevin Hennessy*	*Mark Foley*

The second semi-final between Tipperary and Limerick was played at the Gaelic Grounds on 10 June. Tipperary were expected to win, but their performance was anything but impressive especially in the first forty-five minutes. In fact they owed their victory as much to numerical advantage as to their performance on the field. The Limerick full back Mike Barron was dismissed as early as the seventeenth minute in controversial circumstances, and it wasn't until the final quarter that Tipperary overcame a tiring home team.

Limerick played with obvious confidence and self-assurance from the start and limited Tipperary's scoring chances so much that they got a mere two points from play in the opening half. They had control at centre field where Mike Reale excelled, and Gary Kirby at centre forward along with Shane Fitzgibbon and Ciaran Carey in the corners created many problems for the Tipperary backs. Tipperary added to their woes with poor shooting from the forwards. In spite of the loss of a man, Limerick were still in front 0-11 to 0-8 at the interval.

Tipperary replaced Heffernan and Cormac Bonnar with John Madden and Dinny Ryan, and both were to play significant roles in Tipperary's eventual revival. The pressure began to tell on Limerick, but they were still two points in front before Declan Ryan got Tipperary's opening goal in the forty-second minute. It was to prove the beginning of the end for Limerick. Once Tipperary got in front, their overall performance began to improve and the extra man in the backs made it more difficult for Limerick to score. However, Limerick never collapsed, but their challenge declined steadily after their players became physically and emotionally drained. With Carr taking over control at centre field, Tipperary moved further ahead and a late Mike

Galligan goal was too late to make any difference, with victory going to the champions by 2-20 to 1-17.

TIPPERARY

Ken Hogan

Colm Bonnar	Noel Sheehy	John Heffernan
Conal Bonnar	Bobby Ryan	Paul Delaney

Declan Carr   Joe Hayes (CAPT.)

Michael Cleary	Declan Ryan	John Leahy
Pat Fox	Cormac Bonnar	Nicky English

Subs: John Madden for Heffernan, Dinny Ryan for Cormac Bonnar, Conor Stakelum for Leahy

Tipperary were hoping to win the elusive fourth-in-a-row Munster final when they played Cork at Thurles on 15 July. In a shock defeat, they were beaten by a hungrier and more determined Cork outfit. There was severe criticism of the selectors in the aftermath of the defeat. These criticisms included inaction to remedy weak spots, the removal of key forward Pat Fox at the interval, the failure to include Cormac Bonnar in the starting line-up, and the placing of John Madden at corner back. There was also manager Babs Keating's reference in advance to the impossibility of training a donkey to win a Derby, which gave excellent motivational mileage to the Cork selectors.

Whether these matters decided the outcome or whether it was Cork's excellent performance on the day that was the cause of their victory are in the realm of speculation. Whatever about their role as outsiders, the Cork players showed no uncertainty from the off, charging into the game and playing inspiring hurling for the full seventy minutes. In contrast, Tipperary failed to play up to expectations and only rallied late in the game when it was already beyond reach.

Cork made two changes in their lineout. Seán O'Gorman came on in place of Damien Irwin at left corner back. Teddy McCarthy was replaced at centre field by Brendan O'Sullivan, and in a rearranged forward line John Fitzgibbon came in at corner forward, with Mark Foley moving to the centre.

Tipperary also made a number of changes. John Madden came in at corner back in place of Colm Bonnar. Bobby Ryan was moved back from centre back to left corner to the exclusion of John Heffernan. John Kennedy moved to centre back, with Paul Delaney coming in at left wing back. Conor Stakelum came on at left half-forward, with Johnny Leahy moving to full forward to the exclusion of Cormac Bonnar.

Cork took the game to Tipperary from the throw-in, pointing in less than a minute. The backs coped well with the early pressure, Jim Cashman and Kieran McGuckin being particularly prominent. Brendan O'Sullivan was making his mark at centre field. After eleven minutes they led 0-3 to 0-1. They allowed Tipperary no time to settle, forcing them to deliver the ball hurriedly. In the forward line Tony O'Sullivan,

Mark Foley and Ger Fitzgerald were making trouble for the Tipperary backs.

Tipperary rearranged their forward line with John Leahy coming out to the wing, and their play gradually improved. They were lucky that Cork didn't score goals in the eighteenth and twenty-first minute, and were three points behind when they got their first goal.

It came in the twenty-seventh minute from Michael Cleary, who had moved into the corner. Almost immediately they went in front with a Leahy point, and then English made it two. Then after Cork missed a good chance, Tipperary got a second goal when English touched a high ball from Joe Hayes to the net. However, the effect of this boost and a general improvement in Tipperary's performance was nullified by an opportunist goal from Foley when he connected with a sideline ball from McGuckin. Its timing was perfect and it sent Cork in at half-time in buoyant mood just two points behind, 2-5 to 1-6.

As a result of some admirable striking by Tony O'Sullivan, Cork were level in less than three minutes after the resumption. English restored Tipperary's lead, but it didn't last long as Fitzgibbon got Cork's second goal following good work by Tony O'Sullivan. Cork were now consolidating their superiority, even though there was still half an hour to go.

Tipperary introduced Colm Bonnar, who brought improvement to midfield. Against this, Cork had a very strong grip in defence where Jim Cashman was unbeatable. O'Gorman was moved to full back to reduce the threat of English. The substitution of Dinny

Ryan for Fox failed to improve matters for Tipperary. Mark Foley and Tony O'Sullivan, on the other hand, posed a major threat in the Cork forward line.

Cork enjoyed a six-point lead with twenty minutes remaining, but Tipperary rallied and reduced the lead to two by the fifty-eighth minute. Cork made it three after substitute Casey pointed, but within three minutes it was down to one and Cork looked vulnerable. Foley pointed to move them out of danger.

It was now five minutes from time and Tipperary believed they still had time to recover. But it was Cork who had the final decisive say. Foley goaled following a pass from Hennessy. It was a crushing blow for Tipperary, and worse was to follow in the form of a second from Fitzgibbon with a great solo effort in the sixty-eighth minute. In the course of six minutes Cork had gone from one up to eight up and in an impregnable position.

It was a remarkable finale to a match which did a lot to restore the image of the Munster championship. It re-established Cork in a manner that could hardly have been anticipated in their first round against Kerry or in the semi-final against Limerick. It gave the county their first senior double since 1983 and the chance of further glory in the All-Ireland series. Above all, there was the quiet satisfaction of learning that donkeys do win Derbies!

CORK

Ger Cunningham
(St Finbarr's)

John Considine	Denis Walsh	Seán O'Gorman
(Sarsfields)	(St Catherine's)	(Milford)

Seán McCarthy	Jim Cashman	Kieran McGuckin
(Ballinhassig)	(Blackrock)	(Glen Rovers, capt.)

Pat Buckley   Brendan O'Sullivan
(Milford)   (Valley Rovers)

David Quirke 0-1	Mark Foley 2-7	Tony O'Sullivan 0-5
(Midleton)	(Timoleague)	(Na Piarsaigh)

Gerry Fitzgerald 0-1	Kevin Hennessy 0-1	John Fitzgibbon 2-0
(Midleton)	(Midleton)	(Glen Rovers)

Subs: Tony O'Sullivan (Bishopstown) *for Quirke, Cathal Casey (St Catherine's) 0-1 for Buckley. Also Tom Kingston (Tracton), Pat Kenneally (Newcestown), Christy Connery (Na Piarsaigh), Michael Mullins (Na Piarsaigh), Tomás Mulcahy (Glen Rovers), Damien Irwin (Killeagh), Kevin Kingston (Tracton), John O'Mahony (Ballymartle)*

SELECTORS
Frank Murphy, Fr Michael O'Brien, Denis Hurley,
Martin Coleman, Liam Ó Tuama, Justin McCarthy

TIPPERARY
Ken Hogan
(Lorrha)

John Madden	Noel Sheehy	Bobby Ryan
(Lorrha)	(Silvermines)	(Borrisoleigh)

Conal Bonnar	John Kennedy	Paul Delaney
(Cashel King Cormac's)	(Clonoulty-Rossmore, capt.)	(Roscrea)

Declan Carr   Joe Hayes
(Holycross-Ballycahill)(Clonoulty-Rossmore)

Michael Cleary 1-5	Declan Ryan 0-1	Conor Stakelum 0-2
(Éire Óg, Nenagh)	(Clonoulty-Rossmore)	(Borrisoleigh)

Pat Fox	John Leahy 0-2	Nicky English 1-4
(Éire Óg, Anacarty)	(Mullinahone)	(Lattin-Cullen)

Subs: Dinny Ryan (Newport) for Fox, Colm Bonnar (Cashel King Cormac's) for Carr. Also John Leamy (Golden-Kilfeacle), Cormac Bonnar (Cashel King Cormac's), Donie O'Connell (Killenaule), Conor O'Donovan (Éire Óg, Nenagh), Tony Lanigan (Holycross-Ballycahill), Donie Kealy (Roscrea), John Heffernan (Éire Óg, Nenagh), Pat McGrath (Loughmore-Castleiney)

SELECTORS
Michael Babs Keating, Donie Nealon, Theo English

REFEREE
John Moore
(Waterford)

14

1991: Tipperary come back from the dead

After the disappointment of 1990 Tipperary bounced back the following year. It didn't appear that they would, after losing the league semi-final to Offaly. The Thursday night following the defeat, a training session was agreed, but most of it was taken up with a team talk. It was a time for hard talking, according to manager Babs Keating. The session didn't go as he had hoped: 'A number of the players had a real cut at me and I will always regard this night as one of my best performances in a Tipp dressing room. I let them have their say and I replied without missing a word for about twenty minutes. I reminded each player of his failings. I didn't miss a single turn from previous games. I will always recall one of my co-selectors whispering to me when I finished: "We will win the All-Ireland after that performance." There was dead silence in that dressing room.'

Tipperary avoided the first-round draws and went straight to the semi-final. Limerick and Clare met in the first round at Limerick on 19 May. Limerick won by 0-21 to 1-15, but there wasn't a lot to inspire confidence in their performance. They did enough to win against a Clare side that put up a spirited effort but were handicapped by a lack of scoring power.

Limerick opened well and very quickly had two points on the board. Clare soon wiped out their lead and began to dictate the play. They were four points to the good after twenty minutes and would have been further ahead had their shooting been better. Limerick came back with three points, but Clare were still in front 0-11 to 0-10 at the interval.

On the resumption, Limerick drew level at 0-13 each after five minutes. The game hung in the balance for about ten minutes with neither side scoring. The deadlock was broken by a Kirby point in the forty-ninth minute and Limerick went on to score six points in all with only one in reply from Clare, whose challenge was totally undermined. They did bounce back with a goal from Daffy in the fifty-sixth minute, but though their performance was given a boost, poor shooting let them down and they were three points behind at the final whistle.

On the same day at Killarney, Waterford were pushed to defeat Kerry in the other first-round game. Kerry overcame a bright Waterford start, which saw them lead by 0-3 to 0-1 after ten minutes, to dominate in all sectors of the field and send over a succession of first-half scores to lead by four points, 1-8 to 0-7, at the interval. However, Waterford, helped by good performances from Johnny Brenner at centre field and Billy O'Sullivan at corner forward, gradually clawed their way back into contention during the second half. They were helped by a falling-off in the Kerry performance. Waterford drew level with eleven minutes remaining, and goals by Mossie O'Keeffe and O'Sullivan during that final period sounded the death-knell for the home challenge. The final score was 2-15 to 1-12 in favour of Waterford.

Waterford were a much-changed side for their semi-final meeting with Cork at Thurles on 2 June. A goal by Cork's John Fitzgibbon six minutes from time proved decisive, but Waterford showed admirable spirit and commitment, and only a combination of bad luck and some poor finishing robbed them of victory.

Side by side with Waterford's improved performance was a Cork display well below expectations. This was partly due to Waterford's determination which upset the Cork challenge. As well, Cork had to contend with a poor forward display which yielded only five points in the first half, only one of which was from play. The sides were level at five points each at the interval.

Cork made some changes during the break and had the ball in the net within two minutes of the resumption. Kevin Hennessy was the scorer and Tony O'Sullivan added a point soon after to give Cork a four-point lead. However, within eight minutes Waterford were level with four points from play, two of them from full forward Eddie Nolan, who was causing problems for Richard Browne. It set the scene for a hectic final twenty minutes.

Cork moved Tony O'Sullivan to midfield, and it was to have an impact on the rest of the game. He gave Cork the lead in the fifty-first minute and Pat Buckley followed up with a second point. Waterford came back with two points to level once more in the sixty-first minute. With better finishing they could have been in front.

Cork regained the lead with an O'Sullivan point two minutes later, and immediately afterwards came Fitzgibbon's goal. From the delivery of a high ball from Fitzgerald, it was broken down by Hennessy for Fitzgibbon to finish. It proved the turning point of the game.

Waterford got one point back through Shane Ahearne, and while they were in contention right up to the end after almost three minutes of injury time, they didn't get the opportunities they required to save the match. The final score was 2-10 to 0-13 in favour of Cork.

CORK

Ger Cunningham

Seán O'Gorman	Richard Browne	Denis Walsh
Seán McCarthy	Jim Cashman	Cathal Casey 0-3

Teddy McCarthy   Billy O'Sullivan

Tomás Mulcahy   Mark Foley   Tony O'Sullivan (CAPT.) 0-6

Gerry Fitzgerald   Kevin Hennessy 1-0   John Fitzgibbon 1-0

Subs: John Considine for Walsh, Pat Buckley 0-1 for Foley, Kieran McGuckin for Browne

———◦∞∞∞◦———

Tipperary and Limerick contested the second semi-final at Thurles a week later. The frank team talk after the league semi-final appeared to have worked. Tipperary were much improved and easily accounted for a poor Limerick challenge, further weakened by the sending off of captain, Anthony Carmody, just over thirty minutes into the game for a wild pull on Tipperary forward Michael Cleary. To some it appeared a harsh decision by Waterford referee John Moore, but it followed a series of earlier incidents and he may have felt the need to establish his authority.

Limerick, who lined out without Ciaran Carey, played with the advantage of the breeze and made the early running. At the time they lost Carmody they were leading 0-5 to 0-3, and they were a point in front when Cormac Bonnar rounded Pa Carey and raced away to kick a goal in the thirty-fourth minute. At the break it was 1-5 to 0-7.

Tipperary improved their position by going into a three-point lead soon after the resumption and the sides remained like this until the sixteenth minute of the second half. Then in a matter of minutes the whole complexion of the game changed. Nicky English, now mastering Brian Finn and creating much more room, pointed. Fox and Leahy followed with two more. These scores showed Tipperary at their best and very much in control. They were making the extra man count in the backs where they frustrated Limerick's attempts at scoring. Long before the end the verdict was decided.

When English scored a great goal thirteen minutes from the end, the game was over. This score put the game beyond Limerick's reach. They failed to score for sixteen minutes until Gary Kirby had their last in the sixty-fifth minute. The final score was 2-18 to 0-10.

TIPPERARY

Ken Hogan

Paul Delaney   *Conor O'Donovan*   *Noel Sheehy*

John Madden   *Bobby Ryan*   *John Kennedy*

Declan Carr (CAPT.)   *Joe Hayes*

Michael Cleary 0-5   *Declan Ryan 0-3*   *John Leahy 0-3*

Pat Fox 0-4   *Cormac Bonnar 1-1*   *Nicky English 1-2*

Sub: Michael Ryan for Kennedy

The final between Cork and Tipperary at Páirc Uí Chaoimh on 7 July produced a memorable clash and one of the best contests between the sides for decades. The game exhibited passionate play, skill and excitement and it came down to a last-minute point by

Pat Fox to force a draw. It was an occasion of tremendous atmosphere.

Cork made two changes to the side that lined out for the semi-final. John Considine, who had replaced Denis Walsh at corner back on that occasion, retained his position. Pat Hartnett replaced Teddy McCarthy at centre field. Tipperary made one change with Conal Bonnar coming on in place of John Kennedy at wing back.

Although they won the toss, Tipperary opted to play against the wind. Cork settled quickly, but Tipperary managed to lead by 0-3 to 0-2 after just six minutes. Soon after, Kevin Hennessy goaled and after that Cork were in front for the rest of the game. Two minutes later Ger Fitzgerald had the ball in the net for a second goal following good work by Mark Foley and John Fitzgibbon. At this stage Cork were rampant, taking a score from every attack and hardly wasting a ball.

Tipperary were struggling badly and were having huge problems in their full back line. At the other end the Cork half-back line were holding sway over the Tipperary half-forward line. Cork's superiority was reflected in their third goal by Fitzgerald in the sixteenth minute. This score showed the Cork forwards at their best and highlighted the continued vulnerability of the Tipperary inside back line.

Cork were now seven points clear and in a commanding position. In spite of that Tipperary began to make significant progress in the period to half-time. After Cormac Bonnar made a weak attempt at goal, Leahy, now starting to make his presence felt, had the ball in the Cork net after twenty minutes. At the same time the Tipperary backs began to tighten up. However, the forwards missed scoring opportunities, especially English, who ended the half with only one point to his credit in spite of opportunites for at least two goals. Cork led by 3-5 to 1-7 at the interval.

Tipperary resumed with Noel Sheehy at full back and Michael Ryan at corner, and the change was to make a big improvement in the Tipperary defence. They began to close down the Cork forwards and made it more difficult for them to make progress. The improvement in Tipperary's performance came gradually. Mark Foley, who had destroyed Tipperary the previous year, was closed down at every opportunity.

Tipperary's best efforts received a stunning setback in the fifty-fourth minute when Fitzgibbon got Cork's fourth goal and opened up a seven-point lead once more. Cleary countered with two quick points before substitute, Pat Buckley, scored what proved to be Cork's last point until near the very end.

Entering the last ten minutes, Cork had a six-point lead, and then came Tipperary's best period during which they drew level, only to have Cork regain the lead with a great point by Hennessy from the wing. Following that came the controversial English point, when he lost his hurley and kicked the ball over the bar. The umpire deemed it wide and it took a Fox point to equalise the game just into injury time. Both sides lost opportunities to score during the final pulsating minutes amid the tension and excitement, but the draw was a fitting climax to a tremendous contest.

CORK

Ger Cunningham

John Considine   *Richard Browne*   *Seán O'Gorman*

Seán McCarthy   *Jim Cashman*   *Cathal Casey 0-2*

Brendan O'Sullivan   *Pat Hartnett*

Tomás Mulcahy   *Mark Foley*   *Tony O'Sullivan* (CAPT.) *0-3*

Ger Fitzgerald 2-0   *Kevin Hennessy 1-2*   *John Fitzgibbon 1-2*

Subs: David Quirke for Hartnett, Pat Buckley 0-1 for Brendan O'Sullivan, Teddy McCarthy for Quirke

TIPPERARY

Ken Hogan

Paul Delaney   *Conor O'Donovan*   *Noel Sheehy*

John Madden   *Bobby Ryan*   *Conal Bonnar*

Declan Carr (CAPT.)   *Joe Hayes*

Michael Cleary 0-8   *Declan Ryan 0-1*   *John Leahy 1-1*

Pat Fox 1-3   *Cormac Bonnar 0-1*   *Nicky English 0-1*

Subs: Michael Ryan for O'Donovan, Aidan Ryan 0-1 for Hayes

Whereas a crowd of close to 47,000 packed the Cork venue for the drawn game, an estimated 60,000 spectators filled Semple Stadium for the replay on 21 July. Both sides made changes for the game. Michael

28. *A flare-up between the players in the drawn 1987 Munster final between Cork and Tipperary at Thurles.* (LEFT TO RIGHT): *Gerry Fitzgerald (Cork), Tomás Mulcahy (Cork), Richard Stakelum (Tipperary), Kevin Kingston (Cork), Conor O'Donovan (Tipperary), John Heffernan (Tipperary), Séamus Gibson (Tipperary).* (INPHO)

29. *'Where's the ball gone to?' the faces seem to be saying, in the drawn 1987 Munster final between Cork and Tipperary at Thurles.* (LEFT TO RIGHT): *John McGrath (Tipperary), Denis Mulcahy (Cork), Denis Walsh (Cork), Pat Hartnett (Cork), Pat Fox (Tipperary), Aidan Ryan (Tipperary), Bobby Ryan (Tipperary), Jim Cashman (Cork).* (INPHO)

30. Tipperary captain Richard Stakelum takes the field for extra time at the 1987 Munster final replay at Killarney. (INPHO)

31. *A dramatic picture as Denis Walsh (Cork) catches Nicky English (Tipperary) in the nose in the 1990 Munster final.* (Inpho)

32. *Nicky English (Tipperary) attempts to break through as Seán O'Gorman (Cork) prepares to challenge him in the 1990 Munster final.* (Inpho)

33. *Dinny Ryan (Tipperary) gains possession, pursued by Seán McCarthy (Cork), in the 1990 Munster final at Cork.* (INPHO)

34. *The Tipperary team that won the 1991 Munster final at Thurles.* BACK ROW (LEFT TO RIGHT): *N. Sheehy, M. Ryan, K. Hogan, D. Ryan, J. Madden, D. O'Connell, B. Ryan.* FRONT ROW (LEFT TO RIGHT): *M. Cleary, Cormac Bonnar, Conal Bonnar, D. Carr (capt.), P. Fox, Colm Bonnar, J. Leahy, P. Delaney.* (INPHO)

35. *Noel Sheehy (Tipperary) and Ger Fitzgerald (Cork) contest for a high ball in the 1991 drawn Munster final between Cork and Tipperary at Cork.* (INPHO)

36. *Cormac Bonnar (Tipperary) celebrates the win over Cork with his supporters after the 1991 replayed Munster final victory at Thurles.* (INPHO)

37. *Tipperary manager Babs Keating and selector John O'Donoghue invade the pitch after victory in the 1991 Munster final against Cork at Thurles.* (INPHO)

38. Gary Kirby (Limerick) holds the trophy aloft after victory over Clare in the 1994 Munster final at Thurles. (INPHO)

39. *Limerick supporters celebrate after victory over Clare in the 1994 Munster final at Thurles.* (INPHO)

40. *A determined Ciaran Carey (Limerick) bursts through the tackle by Stephen Sheehy (Clare) in the 1994 Munster final at Thurles.* (INPHO)

41. *The Clare team that made the historic breakthrough by beating Limerick in the 1995 Munster final at Thurles.* BACK ROW (LEFT TO RIGHT): *B. Lohan, M. O'Halloran, C. Clancy, D. Fitzgerald, F. Lohan, S. McMahon, Fergus Tuohy, Ger O'Loughlin.* FRONT ROW (LEFT TO RIGHT): *L. Doyle, P. J. O'Connell, O. Baker, A. Daly (capt.), J. O'Connor, S. McNamara, F. Hegarty.* (INPHO)

42. *A jubilant Clare manager, Ger Loughnane, after victory over Limerick in the 1995 Munster final at Thurles.* (INPHO)

43. *Clare captain Anthony Daly with the trophy, after victory in the 1995 Munster final over Limerick at Thurles.* (INPHO)

44. *Fergus Tuohy (Clare) on the burst in the 1995 Munster final at Thurles, with Tadhg Hayes (Limerick) in pursuit.* (INPHO)

45. *Liam Doyle (Clare) under pressure from Pat Heffernan (Limerick) in the 1995 Munster final at Thurles.* (INPHO)

46. *Colin Lynch (Clare) chased by John Leahy (Tipperary) in the 1997 Munster final at Cork.* (INPHO)

47. *A young Clare supporter celebrating his county's victory over Tipperary in the 1997 Munster final.* (INPHO)

48. *Anthony Daly (Clare) after receiving the trophy from Munster Council chairman, Noel Walsh, following victory over Tipperary in the 1997 Munster final at Cork.* (INPHO)

49. *The Waterford team that defeated Tipperary in the 2002 Munster final at Cork.* BACK ROW (LEFT TO RIGHT): *M. White, J. Murray, K. McGrath, S. Prendergast, S. Brenner, N. Kelly, P. Queally, J. Mullane, E. Murphy, T. Feeney, A. Moloney, D. Shanahan, J. O'Connor, B. Phelan.* FRONT ROW (LEFT TO RIGHT): *P. Flynn, E. McGrath, T. Browne, B. Greene, E. Kelly, B. Flannery, D. Prendergast, P. Fitzgerald, F. Hartley, C. Watt, D. Bennett. (Also in squad but not included in the photograph, M. Walsh.)* (INPHO)

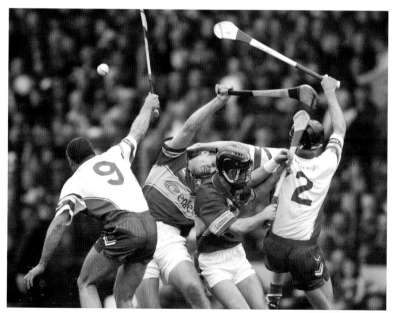

50. *Peter Queally and James Murray (Waterford) compete for possession with Conor Gleeson and Tomás Dunne (Tipperary) in the 2002 Munster final at Cork.* (INPHO)

51. *Tony Browne (Waterford) gets in his puck despite the attentions of Noel Morris (Tipperary) in the 2002 Munster final.* (INPHO)

52. *Eoin McGrath, John Mullane and Eoin Kelly (Waterford) celebrate with the trophy after victory over Tipperary in the 2002 Munster final at Cork.* (INPHO)

53. *Waterford fans at Thurles for the 2004 Munster final against Cork.* (INPHO)

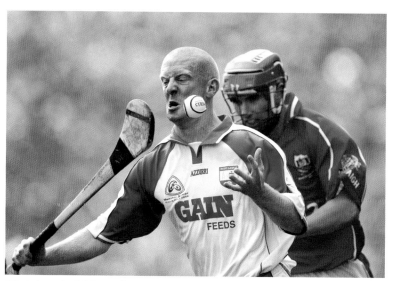

54. *A determined John Mullane (Waterford) attempts to break away from the attentions of Brian Murphy (Cork) in the 2004 Munster final at Thurles.* (INPHO)

55. Ken McGrath (Waterford) celebrates victory over Cork in the 2004 Munster final at Thurles. (INPHO)

56. Dan Shanahan (Waterford) celebrates at the final whistle following victory over Cork in the 2004 Munster final at Thurles. (INPHO)

Ryan came in for the injured Conor O'Donovan, with Noel Sheehy moving to full back. Colm Bonnar replaced Joe Hayes at centre field. With the absence of Nicky English through injury, Donie O'Connell was introduced at centre forward, with Declan Ryan going wing and Michael Cleary corner forward. For Cork, Denis Walsh returned to the full back line in place of John Considine. Seán McCarthy was replaced by Pat Hartnett in the half-back line, with Teddy McCarthy coming in at centre field.

Tipperary started well with the forwards moving smoothly and were three points up after twelve minutes. But then the Cork half-back line clicked into gear, and with Seán O'Gorman playing inspirational hurling on the inside line, the balance of power swung Cork's way as the supply of ball to the Tipperary forwards was cut off. Cork drew level by the eighteenth minute and went ahead when Fitzgibbon found the Tipperary net a minute later. The Cork momentum was halted soon after when Cormac Bonnar set up Michael Cleary for a Tipperary goal. But Cork were back with another goal by Fitzgerald in the twenty-sixth minute and they looked comfortably in control as they led 2-8 to 1-7 at the interval.

Cork continued to grow in stature after the resumption, and when Kevin Hennessy scored a remarkable goal to send Cork into a nine-point lead with twenty-three minutes remaining, it looked as if Tipperary were as good as gone.

What followed was like a dream for every Tipperary supporter at the game or watching it on television. A Joe

Hayes delivery was picked up by Pat Fox, who flicked it past the out-coming Ger Cunningham. A Conal Bonnar free was deflected to the Cork net by Declan Carr. A swooping Aidan Ryan raced past defenders to beat Cunningham for goal number three. Each goal led to a field incursion by jubilant supporters. Michael Cleary added two points to complete one of the greatest recoveries of all time and give Tipperary one of the sweetest of victories by 4-19 to 4-15. They had scored 3-9 to Cork's 1-2 in the final twenty-eight minutes.

The sensation and elation of the victory were vividly caught in the ballad, 'Ó Muirchaertaigh's Miracle', which describes how a group of Tipperary holiday-makers in France on the day picked up the commentary on a bad radio signal at Le Havre, and the transformation of their feelings from the first information that Cork were nine points up to those felt with news of the victory:

One day we heard a miracle like Fatima or Knock,
From Micheál Ó Muircheartaigh — 'Fair play to you auld stock.'

TIPPERARY

Ken Hogan
(Lorrha)

Paul Delaney	*Noel Sheehy*	*Michael Ryan*
(Roscrea)	(Silvermines)	(Upperchurch)
John Madden	*Bobby Ryan 0-2*	*Conal Bonnar*
(Lorrha)	(Borrisoleigh)	(Cashel King Cormac's)

Declan Carr 1-1   Colm Bonnar
(HOLYCROSS-BALLYCAHILL)(CASHEL KING CORMAC'S)

Declan Ryan   Donie O'Connell   John Leahy 0-2
(CLONOULTY-ROSSMORE) (KILLENAULE)   (MULLINAHONE)

Pat Fox 1-5   Cormac Bonnar 0-1   Michael Cleary 1-7
(ÉIRE ÓG, ANACARTY) (CASHEL KING CORMAC'S) (ÉIRE ÓG, NENAGH)

Subs: Aidan Ryan (BORRISOLEIGH) 1-1 for O'Connell, Joe Hayes
(CLONOULTY-ROSSMORE) for Madden. Also Jodie Grace
(TOOMEVARA), Conor Stakelum (BORRISOLEIGH), Michael O'Meara
(TOOMEVARA), Ger O'Neill (CAPPAWHITE), Seán Nealon (BURGESS),
Tony Lanigan (HOLYCROSS-BALLYCAHILL), Nicky English (LATTIN-
CULLEN)

SELECTORS
Michael Babs Keating, Donie Nealon, John O'Donoghue

CORK
Ger Cunningham
(ST FINBARR'S)

Seán O'Gorman   Richard Browne   Denis Walsh
(MILFORD)   (BLACKROCK)   (ST CATHERINE'S)

Cathal Casey 0-1   Jim Cashman 0-3   Pat Hartnett
(ST CATHERINE'S & UCC)(BLACKROCK)   (MIDLETON)

Brendan O'Sullivan   Teddy McCarthy
(VALLEY ROVERS)   (SARSFIELDS)

Tomás Mulcahy 0-1   Mark Foley   Tony O'Sullivan 0-6
(GLEN ROVERS)   (TIMOLEAGUE)   (NA PIARSAIGH, CAPT.)

Ger Fitzgerald 1-2   Kevin Hennessy 1-0   John Fitzgibbon 2-1
(Midleton)   (Midleton)   (Glen Rovers)

Sub: Pat Buckley (Milford) *0-1 for Brendan O'Sullivan. Also Tom Kingston* (Tracton), *John Considine* (Sarsfields), *Kieran McGuckin* (Glen Rovers), *Seán McCarthy* (Ballinhassig), *David Quirke* (Midleton)

SELECTORS
Fr Michael O'Brien, Frank Murphy, Denis Hurley, Martin Coleman, John Gardiner, Gerald McCarthy (trainer)

REFEREE
Terence Murray
(Limerick)

15

CLASSIC
MUNSTER
HURLING
FINALS

1994: Limerick return to Munster glory

There was a series of surprises in the Munster championship of 1994. Tipperary were brilliant in the league final when, without the services of Pat Fox and Nicky English, they waltzed past Galway and seemed set to sweep through Munster. They were certainly expected to beat Clare in the first round and confirm the superiority they had shown in the 1993 championship. The result was very different, with victory going to Clare by a four-point margin in contrast to an eighteen-point defeat the previous year. There was another surprise in the other first-round game when Limerick overcame an eight-point deficit to beat the 1993 Munster champions, Cork, by three points. The final brought Clare and Limerick together, with the former fancied to take their first Munster final since 1932 on the basis of their

success against the same opposition in 1993. Instead, there was another surprise, a sad disappointment for the Banner and a comprehensive victory for the Limerick side.

The first round pitted Clare against Tipperary at the Gaelic Grounds on 29 May. The league champions went into the game with a number of injuries. Joe Hayes, John Leahy and Nicky English were ruled out, and Pat Fox wasn't considered fit enough to start. In spite of these defections from the side, a crowd of only 18,215 seemed to suggest the game was a foregone conclusion.

Clare had other ideas. The huge defeat at the hands of Tipperary the previous year obviously rankled, especially in the light of their earlier victory over Cork. They had not done themselves justice and they believed that the opposition was ripe for the taking. Selector, Ger Loughnane, reflected the feeling in his remarks after the game: 'We had to do something to avenge last year. It was a long wait but, boy, it was worth waiting for. People might have said we were not under pressure, but we were under savage pressure.'

The game wasn't a foregone conclusion until four minutes from time when Tommy Guilfoyle scored his second goal for Clare. It climaxed a contest which was a tame affair over the opening thirty-five minutes and didn't really spring to life until Guilfoyle had his first goal eleven minutes into the second half. Tipperary did the early running and led by 0-6 to 0-2 after twenty-eight minutes, all but one of the six points coming from placed balls. Clare came more into the game during the remaining minutes of the half and were behind 0-7 to 0-5 at the interval.

Clare started the better side in the second half. Great defensive covering, particularly by Anthony Daly and Brian Lohan, good midfield work by Jamesie O'Connor, and a thundering display by P. J. O'Connell in the forwards contributed. However, the game remained close and the sides were still level in the sixty-eighth minute. A Tipperary effort by Pat Fox at this stage went over the bar rather than under, and it was the turning point of the game. A long-range free by Davy Fitzgerald soon after went over the bar, and then came Guilfoyle's clinching goal to give Clare a four-point victory on a scoreline of 2-11 to 0-13.

'There have been a lot of bad days, a few good days, and great days were rare. But today's was definitely one of the greatest', was Loughnane's comment after the game. For manager and Tipperary man, Len Gaynor, it was a bitter-sweet experience: 'I just wanted to see Clare win. I did not want to see Tipp being beaten.'

CLARE

Davy Fitzgerald

Anthony Daly (CAPT.) *Brian Lohan*   *Francis Corey*

John O'Connell   *Seánie McMahon*   *John Chaplin*

Stephen Sheehy   *Damien Considine*

Anthony Neville   *P. J. O'Connell*   *Jamesie O'Connor*

Jim McInerney   *Tommy Guilfoyle*   *Ger O'Loughlin*

Subs: Ger Moroney for Corey, Fergus Tuohy for Neville, Philip Markham for O'Connell

Cork and Limerick played the other first-round game at the Gaelic Grounds the following Sunday. Cork were favourites to come through, but Limerick's victory showed that the wind of change was blowing through Munster hurling. Limerick drew inspiration from the goalkeeping of Joe Quaid, the midfield mastery of Ciaran Carey and the opportunism of full forward Pat Heffernan. It was only the fourth time in twenty-three championship clashes since 1940 that Limerick had beaten Cork, the previous time in the 1980 decider.

This was a game to remember, memorable for some great passages of play, excellent scores, wholehearted endeavour and admirable sportsmanship. Cork made the better start, going three points clear by the eighth minute and getting the first of their goals four minutes later from Mark Mullins. In another four minutes Cork were eight points in front, 2-4 to 0-2, following their second goal by Ger Manley. Not only were Cork getting the scores; they were also dominating the play.

About midway through the half Limerick got a break when a saved twenty-one yard free went out for a 70. When the ball came back in from Ciaran Carey, it was hit to the top of the net by Gary Kirby. This lifted the Limerick display and with Ciaran Carey beginning to dominate at midfield, Kirby becoming more effective and improved performances from T. J. Ryan, Declan Nash, Dave Clarke and Ger Hegarty, Cork were soon on the hind tit. Limerick got their second goal in the twenty-seventh minute, drew level five minutes later and went ahead with a Kirby goal soon after. Cork were now in disarray and they were behind by 3-6 to 2-5 when the break came.

Cork reappeared the better team, were level in the forty-sixth minute, and the lead changed hands for a while after that. Limerick went in front in the fifty-second minute, but then they wasted a number of opportunities and the game hung in the balance for about ten minutes. Then Tomás Mulcahy missed a great goal opportunity, only to have Limerick get one through Pat Heffernan from the puck-out. Carey was now inspirational at centre field, and a high shot from him was flicked to the net by Heffernan to put Limerick in a commanding position. Kevin Murray got through for Cork's fourth goal with a few minutes to go, and it was touch and go during the final thrilling minutes when an Egan chance for the equaliser was just outside the post. The final score was 4-14 to 4-11.

Cork were at a loss to know what happened. Losing the eight-point lead in the first half and going four down before half-time was incomprehensible to them. By contrast, Limerick's joy was boundless. They had beaten the favourites. When they were so far behind in the first half, they hadn't crumbled but came back to level, to go ahead and finally to win. It made all past defeats just vague memories and opened up the vista of a bright future.

LIMERICK
Joe Quaid

John O'Neill	Mike Nash	Stephen McDonagh
David Clarke	Ger Hegarty	Declan Nash
	Ciaran Carey	Mike Houlihan

Frankie Carroll   *Gary Kirby* (CAPT.)   *Mike Galligan*

T. J. Ryan   *Pat Heffernan*   *Damien Quigley*

Subs: Leo O'Connor for Quigley, Donie Flynn for Hegarty

———⊗⊗⊗———

Clare travelled to Tralee on 12 June for the first of the semi-finals against Kerry. It wasn't much of a contest and Clare won easily with double scores, 2-16 to 1-8. They got off to a good start, led by 2-11 to 1-1 at the interval — the Kerry goal was a rather fortuitous effort in the fifteenth minute — and then appeared to sit on their lead, being outscored by their opponents in the second half. In fact the second half was a very scrappy affair in which Clare wasted many scoring opportunities. Clare selector, Fr Willie Walsh, wasn't pleased with the overall display: 'We are always glad to win, but our general play in the second half wasn't good enough. We wouldn't win a Munster final with that type of form. But we came to win and we did that.'

Clare made a few changes to the team that played against Tipperary. Liam Doyle was on at left corner back in place of Francis Corey, Christy Chaplin came in at centre field in place of Damien Considine, and Fergus Tuohy replaced Tommy Guilfoyle at full forward.

———⊗⊗⊗———

The second semi-final was played at Thurles on 19 June and Limerick were anything but pleased with their victory over Waterford, winning by 2-14 to 2-12. In fact it was more in relief than jubilation that they greeted the end of the game.

Limerick never managed to play with the same flair or authority as they did when surprising Cork in the first round, and there were long periods when they looked extremely vulnerable. Waterford led on two occasions during the first quarter, but after that Limerick were never headed. Backed by a strong breeze, they had a purple patch between the seventeenth and twentieth minutes when they managed to score a goal and four points without reply. After that they squandered some good chances but were in front by 2-10 to 1-6 at the interval.

With the wind in their favour in the second half, Waterford scored four points during a ten-minute period but wasted many opportunities also. Limerick were in even greater difficulty getting a score and they went twenty-two minutes before getting their first score in the half. They were to get three more before the final whistle as they lived precariously, helped as much by Waterford's profligacy as their own ability. They were probably lucky that Waterford failed to get their second goal until injury time and were relieved when the final whistle sounded and they were in front by 2-14 to 2-12.

Limerick lined out with a changed inside back line from their first-round game against Cork. Stephen McDonagh switched corners, and Joe O'Connor and Donie Flynn replaced John O'Neill and Mike Nash.

The Clare-Limerick Munster clash at Thurles on 10 July was only the ninth final in the history of the championship without Cork or Tipperary. Although Limerick were to lord it, Clare were the favourites going into the game. They had beaten Cork in 1993 and although beaten badly by Tipperary in the final, had come back in 1994 to reverse the result. The time seemed right for the historic breakthrough. Instead, they put up a poor show in the first half and collapsed under a barrage of Limerick scores after the interval. Their two goals, which gave a gloss to the final result, didn't come until the final eight minutes when Limerick's victory was already assured.

The first half was competitive enough for about two-thirds of its duration. Both sets of backs had the edge on their opponents, with Anthony Daly and Seánie McMahon doing well for Clare. As well, Christy Chaplin won the honours over Ciaran Carey at midfield. But this good work was being wasted by the failure of the Clare forwards to utilise their possession.

Gradually Limerick began to impose themselves with Carey becoming more prominent and Frankie Carroll and Mike Galligan moving well in the forwards. Dave Clarke also moved into a higher gear at wing back. They went three points in front by the fifteenth minute. However, Clare responded and had drawn level at six points each by the twenty-first minute. In fact this was to be the best period of Clare's performance.

In the next few minutes Limerick went two points in front. Clare had a number of wides, the most costly of which was a goal chance from Andrew Whelan. A number of switches were made to try and counteract the influence of Ciaran Carey, but they weren't a success. Limerick had begun to establish control before half-time and they went in leading 0-11 to 0-7.

Limerick resumed as they left off and firmly established their grip on the game. They had some great points, especially from Mike Galligan. The more the gap widened on the scoreboard the more Clare's chances of victory disappeared. Yet Clare twice went close to goaling in the early minutes, first when Stephen Sheehy had a low shot saved by Joe Quaid and then, from the resultant 70, when O'Loughlin had the ball at his feet and failed to kick it into the net.

In the aftermath of defeat Clare could look back to these and other goal misses and take consolation in the thought that the result might have been different, had one or more of these opportunities been converted. But there was no such consolation on the day.

After fifteen minutes of play Limerick had opened an eleven-point margin and the game was as good as over as a contest. Clarke grew more and more in stature at wing back. Carey controlled the play in the middle of the field and Houlihan, who had a powerful second half, added to Limerick's dominance. In the forwards Galligan hit five points from play and Gary Kirby was unerring with the placed ball.

Try as they might, Clare had no answer to Limerick's sustained onslaught. Anthony Daly did some great work after switching to centre back and P. J. O'Connell and Jim McInerney tried hard in the forwards. But goal-scoring chances weren't taken, with the exception of a close-in free by Cyril Lyons in the sixty-second minute and a second goal from Tommy Guilfoyle some minutes later. They were too little, too late.

The final score was 0-25 to 2-10 in a game that was lacking in any real excitement. There was little to cheer about for the neutrals in the crowd of 43,638 in what was a very one-sided game. It was Limerick's day as they took their seventeenth title. They dominated the game from the word go. They were first to the ball and their forwards took their scores superbly. Their victory upset the forecasts, and Clare were left wondering what they had to do to make the historic breakthrough.

LIMERICK

Joe Quaid
(FEOHANAGH)

Stephen McDonagh *Mike Nash*   *Joe O'Connor*
(BRUREE)   (SOUTH LIBERTIES) (BALLYBROWN)

David Clarke   *Ger Hegarty*   *Declan Nash*
(KILMALLOCK) (OLD CHRISTIANS) (SOUTH LIBERTIES)

Ciaran Carey 0-2 *Mike Houlihan*
(PATRICKSWELL) (KILMALLOCK)

Frankie Carroll 0-2 *Gary Kirby 0-9* *Mike Galligan 0-7*
(GARRYSPILLANE) (PATRICKSWELL, CAPT.) (CLAUGHAUN)

T. J. Ryan 0-1 *Pat Heffernan 0-2* *Damien Quigley 0-2*
(GARRYSPILLANE) (BLACKROCK) (NA PIARSAIGH)

Subs: John Roche (CROAGH KILFINNY) *for Heffernan, Michael Wallace* (GLENROE) *for Ryan. Also Tom Hennessy* (KILMALLOCK),

John O'Neill (BLACKROCK), Donie Flynn (KILLEEDY), Brian Finn (BRUFF), Donal Barry (KILMALLOCK), Ger Galvin (FEENAGH-KILMEEDY), Leo O'Connor (CLAUGHAUN)

SELECTORS

Tom Ryan (MANAGER), Liam Lenihan (TOURNAFULLA), Rory Kiely (FEENAGH-KILMEEDY), Dave Mahedy (TRAINER)

CLARE

Davy Fitzgerald
(SIXMILEBRIDGE)

Anthony Daly	Brian Lohan	Liam Doyle
(CLARECASTLE, CAPT.)	(WOLFE TONES)	(BODYKE)

John O'Connell	Seánie McMahon	John Chaplin
(SIXMILEBRIDGE)	(ST JOSEPH'S, DOORA-BAREFIELD)	(SIXMILEBRIDGE)

Stephen Sheehy 0-1	Christy Chaplin 0-1
(CLARECASTLE)	(SIXMILEBRIDGE)

Andrew Whelan 0-1	P. J. O'Connell	Jamesie O'Connor 0-3
(ST JOSEPH'S, DOORA-BAREFIELD)	(O'CALLAGHAN'S MILLS)	(ST JOSEPH'S, DOORA-BAREFIELD)

Jim McInerney 0-1	Tommy Guilfoyle 1 0	Ger O'Loughlin 0-3
(TULLA)	(FEAKLE)	(CLARECASTLE)

Subs: Francis Corey (ÉIRE ÓG) for John O'Connell, Cyril Lyons (RUAN) 1-0 for John Chaplin. Also Noel Considine (CLARECASTLE), Ger Moroney (O'CALLAGHAN'S MILLS), Pat Markham (CLOONEY), Fergus Tuohy (CLARECASTLE), Ciaran O'Neill (ST JOSEPH'S, DOORA-BAREFIELD), Ken Morrissey (CLARECASTLE), Eamonn Taffe (TUBBER)

SELECTORS
Len Gaynor (MANAGER), Fr Willie Walsh, Ger Loughnane

REFEREE
Willie Barrett

(TIPPERARY)

16

1995: Clare's historic breakthrough

C lare won the Munster senior hurling final in 1995 after a long wait. No county had had so many disappointments in a long hurling history, particularly in the decades stretching back to 1955. Beaten in eleven finals over the period, Clare supporters had come to believe that a Munster final would never come to the Banner county.

There wasn't much to presage the events of 1995. Admittedly Clare had defeated Cork in the 1993 championship, and Tipperary in 1994, but they had been humiliated in the final by Limerick that same year. Again, after an impressive showing in the 1994/95 National League, losing only one game on their way to the final, they failed against Kilkenny in a game that showed a big difference in class between the two sides.

Somehow the manager, Ger Loughnane, was able to see some light at the end of the tunnel, but few after the defeat were inclined to believe his prediction: 'We will win the Munster championship this summer.'

Loughnane had taken over as manager after serving for two years under Len Gaynor. In fact he had been impatient to be at the helm and had appointed Mike McNamara and Tony Considine to his management team. The team got together for their first session on Tuesday after the 1994 All-Ireland. Between then and Christmas they were put through the most gruelling of regimes, so gruelling in fact that Liam Doyle recalls travelling back from a training session with Mike McNamara and refusing to talk to him, he hated him so much! In retrospect, Doyle sees these sessions as important builders of confidence levels. As their physical preparation improved the players learned that they could keep going longer and this helped them to perform better. All the while it was repeated to them that they were training for the following September and for winning an All-Ireland. Doyle admits that they didn't buy into the propaganda at first, retaining the strong memories of their failures in previous championships, but gradually they came to believe in themselves and they showed it against Cork.

Cork and Kerry opened the championship with a first-round meeting at Tralee on Saturday, 20 May. For a few fleeting moments it looked as though Kerry might cause a surprise, but as Kerry team manager John Meyler put it: 'In the end Cork drilled too many holes in us and we were unable to plug the gaps.'

In fact it was well into the second half before Cork managed to kill off the Kerry challenge. Cork raced into an early lead and were ten points to two in front after twenty-five minutes. But they failed to register a score during the remainder of the half, while Kerry added four points to leave them trailing by four, 0-10 to 0-6, at the interval. Kerry resumed full of confidence, but it didn't last long and gradually Cork established their grip on the game. Good goalkeeping by Healy prevented Cork from going further ahead, and he was unfortunate to concede the only goal of the game in injury time. In the end Cork were easy winners by 1-22 to 0-12, even though Johnny Clifford wasn't impressed with the team's topsy-turvy form: 'We have this disconcerting habit of letting things go when we are on top. We fail to punish our opponents and that is one flaw that must be remedied if we are to progress in the championship.'

Tipperary were in top gear against Waterford in the other first-round game, which was played the same weekend at Páirc Uí Chaoimh. A mere 15,000 spectators saw Tipperary outclass their opponents. With the exception of Damien Byrne at full back and Stephen Frampton, Waterford did not possess the skill and craft to match Tipperary's expertise.

Tipperary opened brightly and were in front by 0-9 to 0-3 after twenty minutes. The Tipperary backs, especially Noel Sheehy, George Frend and Raymie Ryan, gave their opponents few opportunities, and by half-time the lead was extended to 0-12 to 0-5. At this stage a sense of the inevitable hung over the proceedings. On the resumption Tipperary widened the gap and the only light for Waterford appeared in the forty-seventh minute when centre forward Ger Harris pounced for a goal, which reduced the deficit to six points. However, it was only a brief respite before the dam gates opened and Tipperary pushed on to a comprehensive victory by 4-23 to 1-11.

In spite of the wide margin of victory, Tipperary manager Fr Tom Fogarty wasn't entirely pleased. He felt that the team 'should have pulled away much earlier' and he wasn't very impressed with the finishing in the attack nearing half-time and again early in the second half. 'We over-elaborated a bit too much at times.'

Clare snatched victory from Cork in the Munster semi-final at the Gaelic Grounds on 4 June. It was one of the sweetest of victories for a county that had been on the receiving end of such thefts in the past. Cork, it seemed, were destined to win when Kevin Murray goaled in the last minute, but Clare, displaying an almost fanatical belief in themselves, responded with a superb Ollie Baker goal forty seconds into injury time. And it wasn't over yet as a great shot for the equaliser by Alan Browne came back off an upright in the dying moments.

No wonder Clare manager Ger Loughnane was ecstatic afterwards: 'This was without doubt the greatest victory Clare have achieved in all my time of being involved with hurling in the county. Certainly no Clare team in the modern era fought so bravely or with so much heart.'

Incredibly, only 14,000 people were present and the diminished number seemed justified with the poor quality of the game until the pulsating final quarter. Until then the game was a sad advertisement for hurling, with an almost criminal waste of possession on both sides: Clare had twenty wides in the course of the hour, and Cork fifteen. There were few scores in the opening twenty minutes and the sides were level before Cork opened up a gap with an Alan Browne goal in the twenty-seventh minute. Another followed from Ger Manley a few minutes later, so that Cork retired with a lead of 2-4 to 0-7.

Cork went further ahead after the resumption but Clare, playing now with greater conviction, gradually worked their way back into the game and drew level in the fifty-fifth minute. However, great work by their backs, especially Liam Doyle, was squandered by poor shooting by the forwards. The game hung in the balance until Mark Mullins broke the stalemate with two points, following a spell of seventeen minutes without a score for Cork. They went further ahead with a third point by Murray.

Ger O'Loughlin revived Clare with a marvellous goal and P. J. O'Connell edged them back in front with a point. Then came Murray's goal after an opening was created by Mullins. It looked a winner until Baker finished a Fergus Tuohy sideline shot to the net, and then Browne was unlucky not to force a replay.

Shortly after the game, Cork manager Johnny Clifford announced his retirement: 'I have done my best for Cork hurling, but unfortunately it was not good enough on this occasion.' He added, 'We had our chances to win but inexperience probably proved to be our downfall in the end. We conceded what I would term a soft goal from a Clare sideline puck at the end, and that was the killer blow.'

In contrast, there was jubilation in the Clare camp. According to Loughnane the victory signalled an important change in the status of Clare hurling: 'In the past any Clare team going in at half-time trailing by three points and having played with the wind in the first half would have flopped, but not this present side, who did what I asked of them — to fight to the end regardless of what way things were going for them.'

CLARE
Davy Fitzgerald

Michael O'Halloran   Brian Lohan   Liam Doyle

Anthony Daly (CAPT.)   Seánie McMahon   John Chaplin

Stephen Sheehy   Jamesie O'Connor

Fergus Tuohy   P. J. O'Connell   Fergus Hegarty

Jim McInerney   Conor Clancy   Ger O'Loughlin

Subs: Ollie Baker for Sheedy, Frank Lohan for Chaplin, Stephen McNamara for McInerney

Although Limerick were the defending Munster

champions, Tipperary were popular favourites going into the second Munster semi-final at Páirc Uí Chaoimh on 18 June. Their comprehensive defeat of Waterford in the first round, a highly vaunted forward line and their record of success stretching back to 1981 against the opposition, made them appear likely winners.

From early on Limerick looked to be very much up for the game. T. J. Ryan was confident in attack while Ciaran Carey was dominant at centre back. Seán O'Neill was also performing impressively at centre field. As well, Gary Kirby's great display — he was to score nine points from placed balls and three from play — was to be a decisive factor. On the other side, the Tipperary forward line was not performing as expected against an alert Limerick back line.

The opening half was a close and dogged affair with little fluid hurling. Tipperary had to wait until the twenty-eighth minute to go in front, and they were anything but impressive with a lead of 0-9 to 0-7 at the interval. Limerick drew level soon after the resumption, and for a long period the sides were level. Then Limerick went two points in front, only to be pulled back to one with seven minutes to go. Soon after, Kirby made it two again, and again it was pegged back to one with a Cleary point just on time. In extra time Pat Fox was denied an equaliser by a great block-down by Mike Nash, and then Declan Ryan, from a good position near midfield, hit a shot harmlessly wide to leave the final score 0-16 to 0-15 in Limerick's favour.

Limerick manager Tom Ryan was well pleased with

his charges: 'The character of the side was seen in the closing minutes as Tipp threw everything at them. We needed this victory to banish the All-Ireland defeat of last year from our system and we can now look forward to the Munster final in a couple of weeks' time.'

For Tipperary there was no consolation. In the opinion of Fr Tom Fogarty they were defeated because of too many second-half wides. Also, the absence of Michael Ryan and Paul Delaney through suspension upset the rhythm of the team.

LIMERICK

Joe Quaid

Stephen McDonagh	*Mike Nash*	*Declan Nash*
David Clarke	*Ciaran Carey*	*Turlough Herbert*

Mike Houlihan (CAPT.)   *Seán O'Neill*

Frankie Carroll	*Gary Kirby*	*Mike Galligan*
T. J. Ryan	*Pat Heffernan*	*Damien Quigley*

Subs: Mark Foley for Carroll, Shane O'Neill for Heffernan,
Mike Reale for Houlihan

Clare were playing in their third Munster final in succession when they turned out against Limerick at Thurles on 9 July. In the previous two they had been badly beaten, as they had been in the league final three months earlier. According to Clare coach Mike

McNamara, they kept the talk simple before the game: 'Right lads, it's a Munster final and ye have enough of them lost, so go out now and do whatever it takes.'

And they did just that. Full of courage, commitment and conviction, they fought with passionate intensity and fanatical determination to end one of the longest hurling famines. In doing so they finally laid to rest the 'curse of Biddy Early', which was reputed to hang like an albatross over the fortunes of Clare hurling for more than sixty years. The victory was a comprehensive one with nine points separating the sides on a scoreline of 1-17 to 0-11 when the final whistle sounded.

Clare made a number of changes to the side that defeated Cork. Frank Lohan, who appeared as a sub in that game, came in at left corner back. Liam Doyle went out to right wing back in place of Anthony Daly, who moved to the left wing in place of John Chaplin. Ollie Baker replaced Stephen Sheehy at centre field and Stephen McNamara took over the right corner forward spot from Jim McInerney. In contrast, Limerick lined out with the same team that played against Tipperary.

Played in sweltering conditions and with a ferocious intensity, Clare knocked Limerick, who were no match for the vigour and purpose of their opponents, completely out of their stride from the opening minutes. Tackling furiously and prepared to mix it physically, they succeeded in stifling the superior skills of the Limerickmen with bone-crunching tackles. In spite of this onslaught, Limerick led by five points to two after twenty-one minutes. But they also missed opportunities. As well, they had to contend with a powerful Clare half-back line that reduced their scoring opportunities considerably. Clare began to dominate, getting to grips at centre field and P. J. O'Connell totally upsetting the usually dominant Ciaran Carey. Less well-known Clare players also came good to give the team a rampant performance. Limerick's problems were aggravated in the twenty-eighth minute when goalkeeper Davy Fitzgerald came up the field to crash a penalty to the Limerick net. It was to form the basis of Clare's lead of 1-5 to 0-7 at the interval.

A sign of things to come was a brilliant point by P. J. O'Connell soon after the resumption, which boosted Clare still more. For a brief period Limerick regained their momentum with two points from Kirby, but they were unable to sustain it against the might of Lohan at full back, as well as a dominant Clare half-back line and centre field.

Instead, Clare had three points from Jamesie O'Connor, O'Connell and McMahon with a huge free. Then to aggravate Limerick's woe, corner forward Damien Quigley kicked the ball wide with the goal at his mercy. There were still twenty minutes left, but this was Limerick's last chance.

Clare took over completely and Limerick had no answer to their fiercely combative spirit and controlled aggression. In the closing quarter they played out of their skins and copper-fastened victory with an avalanche of scores. The final tally was 1-17 to 0-11, a comprehensive victory of nine points.

The scenes at Semple Stadium after the final whistle were incredible. Thousands of Clare supporters poured on to the field and stayed there for a long time, not only to greet their heroes and watch the presentation but to savour the strangeness of it all, a Clare victory after sixty-three years and so many defeats. Adding to the Clare occasion was the fact that the chairman of the Munster Council who made the presentation was himself a Clareman, Noel Walsh. He had the honour of presenting the cup to captain Anthony Daly. The celebrations only began at Semple Stadium; they were to continue all the way to Clare and around the county later.

There was universal joy at the Clare victory. They had come a long way, along a hard road, and nobody with the possible exception of Limerick, who were hoping to reverse the previous year's defeat in the All-Ireland, begrudged them their victory. A well-behaved and disciplined bunch of players, the Clare team set standards of behaviour and attitude that were a credit to them and their management. As well, they had a larger than life manager with a messianic streak.

CLARE

Davy Fitzgerald 1-0
(SIXMILEBRIDGE)

Michael O'Halloran	*Brian Lohan*	*Frank Lohan*
(SIXMILEBRIDGE)	(WOLFE TONES)	(WOLFE TONES)

Liam Doyle	*Seánie McMahon 0-1*	*Anthony Daly*
(BODYKE)	(ST JOSEPH'S, DOORA-BAREFIELD)	(CLARECASTLE, CAPT.)

Ollie Baker	*Jamesie O'Connor 0-6*
(ST JOSEPH'S, DOORA-BAREFIELD)	(ST JOSEPH'S, DOORA-BAREFIELD)

Fergus Tuohy 0-1   P. J. O'Connell 0-4   Fergus Hegarty 0-1
(CLARECASTLE)   (O'CALLAGHAN'S MILLS)   (KILNAMONA)

Stephen McNamara 0-1   Conor Clancy 0-2   Ger O'Loughlin 0-1
(ÉIRE ÓG)   (KILMALEY)   (CLARECASTLE)

Subs: Jim McInerney (TULLA) *for Tuohy, Cyril Lyons* (RUAN) *for Clancy. Also Eamonn Taaffe* (TUBBER), *Ger Moroney* (O'CALLAGHAN'S MILLS), *Alan Neville* (CLARECASTLE), *John Chaplin* (SIXMILEBRIDGE), *Christy Chaplin* (SIXMILEBRIDGE), *Ken Morrissey* (CLARECASTLE), *Brian Quinn* (TULLA), *Lorcan Hassett* (ST JOSEPH'S, DOORA-BAREFIELD), *Damien Garrihy* (WOLFE TONES)

LIMERICK
Joe Quaid
(FEOHANAGH)

Stephen McDonagh   Mike Nash   Declan Nash
(BRUREE)   (SOUTH LIBERTIES)   (SOUTH LIBERTIES)

David Clarke   Ciaran Carey   Turlough Herbert
(KILMALLOCK)   (PATRICKSWELL)   (AHANE)

Mike Houlihan   Seán O'Neill
(KILMALLOCK, CAPT.)   (MURROE)

Frankie Carroll 0-1   Gary Kirby 0-6   Mike Galligan 0-3
(GARRYSPILLANE)   (PATRICKSWELL)   (CLAUGHAUN)

T. J. Ryan   Pat Heffernan 0-1   Damien Quigley
(GARRYSPILLANE)   (BLACKROCK)   (NA PIARSAIGH)

Subs: Tadhg Hayes (DOON) *for Herbert, Brian Tobin* (MUNGRET) *for Carroll, Donal Barry* (KILMALLOCK) *for Hayes. Also Tom Hennessy*

(Kilmallock), *Michael Reale* (Bruff), *Mark Foley* (Adare), *Shane O'Neill* (Na Piarsaigh), *Séamus Murphy* (Bruree), *Aidan Frawley* (Bruree)

SELECTORS

Tom Ryan (manager), *Rory Kiely* (Feenagh-Kilmeedy), *Liam Lenihan* (Tournafulla), *Dave Mahedy* (trainer)

REFEREE

Johnny McDonnell
(Tipperary)

17

1997: Clare come back with a vengeance

After their great victory over Limerick in the 1995 Munster final, Clare were brought very much down to earth in the 1996 championship. Being everyone's favourites to repeat the success, they caught a Tartar in a much-renewed and invigorated Limerick in the Munster semi-final, going down 1-13 to 0-15 as a result of a memorable point by Ciaran Carey in the second minute of added time. In the final four minutes of a game which seemed headed in Clare's direction, Limerick pulled back a three-point deficit and transformed it into a one-point victory. For Clare the result was a disaster, caused by an accumulation of problems such as failing to translate territorial advantage into scores, trivial errors and a failure to extend their lead beyond three points when chances went a-begging. They were determined not to be caught again.

Clare commenced their 1997 championship campaign with a comprehensive win over Kerry in a first-round game at Ennis. The result was expected, with Clare going into the game as overwhelming favourites, and they showed by their performance just why. Kerry started brightly, got the first score and were even level after eleven minutes, but then the screw of Clare superiority turned inexorably. By half-time Clare led 2-11 to 1-4, and while Kerry never gave up, the Banner county showed they were a class apart, adding 1-13 as against 0-2 for Kerry during the second half, to leave the final score 3-24 to 1-6 in Clare's favour.

CLARE

Davy Fitzgerald

Michael O'Halloran   Brian Lohan   Brian Quinn

Liam Doyle   Seánie McMahon   Anthony Daly (CAPT.)

Colin Lynch   David Forde

Jamesie O'Connor   Conor Clancy   P. J. O'Connell

Niall Gilligan   Ger O'Loughlin   Brian Murphy

Subs: Fergus Tuohy for O'Connor, Christy Chapman for Forde

Clare's next game, against Cork in the semi-final at

Limerick on 8 June, was a much more difficult contest. Surprisingly, the attendance was a mere 23,000. Cork, who were overwhelmed by Limerick the previous year, were a much-improved side and gave Clare a fright. Clare were in obvious difficulty at the break when they led by 0-9 to 0-8 after playing with the wind. All over the field Cork were highly competitive and weren't giving Clare any time to get into a winning rhythm. Bold measures were required if they aimed to win.

Clare made some switches at the interval, the most important being replacing Niall Gilligan and Conor Clancy with Stephen McNamara and David Forde. Positional switches were also made, the most effective being that of Ger O'Loughlin to full forward. The Clare half-back line stood up to a lot of pressure from Ger Cunningham's puck-outs with the wind. As well, Seánie McMahon pointed three long-range frees which had an impact on the game.

A point by O'Loughlin immediately after the resumption lifted Clare and set them on the road to victory, but it took a late goal by Stephen McNamara to secure success over a very determined Cork, who still had fight left in them after this upset. It took a great save by Fitzgerald from Seánie McGrath to frustrate an injury-time rally.

The Clare manager, Ger Loughnane, breathed a sigh of relief after the victory: 'Cork were back to their brilliant best and all the fears we harboured about them were fully realised in the first half when they really put it up to us. The pressure was fierce, much greater than any All-Ireland final, and things did not look too good at half-time when we led by only a point when playing with the wind. Our backs were to the wall and for many of us our hurling lives were on the line. I asked the lads to make a vow to go out and do their level best to turn in their best ever thirty-five minutes of hurling. That was how precarious our situation was. Thankfully their response was both positive and magnificent and the character they showed in gradually wearing down Cork was admirable in the extreme.'

CLARE

Davy Fitzgerald

Michael O'Halloran   Brian Lohan   Frank Lohan

Liam Doyle   Seánie McMahon   Anthony Daly (CAPT.)

Denis Baker   Colin Lynch

Fergus Tuohy   P. J. O'Connell   Jamesie O'Connor

Niall Gilligan   Conor Clancy   Ger O'Loughlin

Subs: Stephen McNamara for Gilligan, David Forde for Clancy, Andrew Whelan for O'Loughlin

Tipperary, who had a bye to the semi-final, played Limerick at Thurles on 15 June before more than twice the number of spectators that turned up at the Gaelic Grounds the previous Sunday. Limerick came into the game with confidence, having scored an impressive win over Waterford in the first round. They started well, matched Tipperary in most aspects of the game, and traded scores with them. In fact during the opening twenty minutes each of the opening five points for one side was matched by the other.

After this Tipperary were to make rapid progress as Limerick's challenge was to be undermined by a combination of weak forward play and poor finishing. Tipperary's progress was reflected in the improved performance by Declan Ryan at centre forward, where he began to get the better of Ciaran Carey. Kevin Tucker and Tommy Dunne too were more prominent, while Cleary began to pose a greater threat. This improvement paid off in more scores, and by the interval Tipperary were in front by 1-8 to 0-8, the goal coming from Cleary who kicked the ball past Quaid after the Limerick goalkeeper had blocked down a powerful shot from Leahy.

Limerick brought in Pat Heffernan at full forward in the second half, and soon after the resumption Frankie Carroll replaced the injured Ollie Moran. The rearranged forward line began to exert more pressure during the opening fifteen minutes but, critically, could register only two scores while Tipperary had five during that period.

As well as performing well in the forwards, Tipperary were also inspirational in defence, especially Raymie Ryan who gave a stylish performance. The more the game progressed, the more inevitable the outcome became, and when the final whistle sounded Tipperary were well in front on a scoreline of 1-20 to 0-13. Limerick's two big stars, Ciaran Carey and Gary Kirby, had not performed with their usual prominence.

TIPPERARY

Brendan Cummins

Paul Shelly	*Noel Sheehy*	*Michael Ryan*
Raymie Ryan	*Colm Bonnar*	*Conor Gleeson* (CAPT.)

Aidan Butler   *John Leahy*

Kevin Tucker	*Declan Ryan*	*Tommy Dunne*
Liam Cahill	*Michael Cleary*	*Philip O'Dwyer*

Subs: Brendan Carroll for Butler, Conal Bonnar for Raymie Ryan

There was plenty of discussion on the venue for the Munster final with three possible locations, Cork, Limerick and Thurles. As the Gaelic Grounds had limited capacity, it was ruled out. Because Clare did not have a venue sufficiently large to enter into a home and away arrangement with Tipperary, Thurles was also ruled out. So Cork it was, and the date was fixed for 6 July.

Clare had never beaten Tipperary in a Munster final; they had in fact lost four finals to them, so there was a special edge to this encounter. It was a very important one for Clare; their progress would be measured by the result. Manager Ger Loughnane made it clear the game was all about 'winning respect'.

While the greater experience and tradition of

Tipperary were expected to give them some advantage on the occasion, it was Clare who rose to the occasion. Coming into the game the major problem for Clare was the efficiency of their forwards: they hadn't been matching the performance of their backs or, to a lesser extent, their centre field. As it transpired the forwards came up trumps. They produced a match-winning performance which, combined with another great display by their defence and a level of dominance at centre field, could not have been anticipated. Tipperary struggled to match it, never came near mastering it, and yet they might have got an equalising goal in the last minute had John Leahy not uncharacteristically missed in front of the goal.

This final had another interesting dimension as a result of a decision taken at the 1996 Congress. The delegates decided that the runners-up in the Munster and Leinster finals would, on a two-year experimental basis, be permitted to enter All-Ireland quarter-finals, where they would be seeded and drawn to play against either the Connacht or Ulster winners. Any speculation that this 'backdoor' chance would dilute the intensity of the exchanges in a Munster final proved unfounded.

The first twenty minutes of the game at Páirc Uí Chaoimh revealed much about the teams and the possible outcome of the game. There was evidence of Clare's greater potential as well as serious flaws in the Tipperary side. Clare were moving well in attack with Fergus Tuohy and P. J. O'Connell particularly prominent. Conversely, their opposites in the Tipperary half-back line, Colm Bonnar and Raymie Ryan, were in difficulties.

As well, John Leahy was making little contribution at midfield, where Colin Lynch was on top. The Tipperary attack was struggling, with Michael Cleary at full forward no match for Brian Lohan. Poor shooting by Philip O'Dwyer and Liam Cahill saw good opportunities for goals wasted.

After the early exchanges Clare took control and scored eight points without reply to move to 0-10 to 0-2 in front after twenty-seven minutes. Tipperary were in disarray. At this stage the pattern of the contest changed as Tipperary gradually came back into the game. Tommy Dunne moved to centre field and made his presence felt. Declan Ryan began to make an impact, and John Leahy inspired his colleagues with two magnificent points from play. Having failed to raise a flag for over twenty minutes, Tipperary scored six points in the closing nine minutes. Although Clare also got three, the margin of 0-13 to 0-8 at the interval was not insurmountable for Tipperary. On the other hand it didn't reflect the true extent of Clare's superiority.

Tipperary resumed well with the introduction of Aidan Flanagan. It was now Clare who came under pressure as Tommy Dunne and Kevin Tucker hit two points apiece, and Declan Ryan levelled the score at 0-13 each seven minutes after the restart.

At this stage the pendulum swung Clare's way once again. Seánie McMahon landed a huge free and the Clare players began to reassert themselves all over the field. David Forde, who had replaced Stephen McNamara, scored a point and then followed up with a goal, tilting the game Clare's way. Jamesie O'Connor sent over two more points as Clare continued on a roll. There was no doubt who was in charge.

In the closing period Tipperary clawed their way back and outscored Clare by five points to one during the last ten minutes. They might have grabbed a sensational draw had Leahy connected with the sliotar from close range, but it would have been a travesty of justice as Clare's winning margin should have been greater.

There was an interesting postscript to the final. As a result of the Congress decision of 1996, the sides went on to meet in the All-Ireland final. It was the first time in the history of the competition that two teams from the same province met in the national decider. It generated enormous interest, and at the end of an exciting game which saw a spectacular save by Clare's Davy Fitzgerald, Clare confirmed their superiority with a one-point winning margin, 0-20 to 2-13.

CLARE

Davy Fitzgerald
(SIXMILEBRIDGE)

Michael O'Halloran   *Brian Lohan*   *Frank Lohan*
(SIXMILEBRIDGE)   (WOLFE TONES)   (WOLFE TONES)

Liam Doyle   *Seánie McMahon 0-3*   *Anthony Daly*
(BODYKE)   (ST JOSEPH'S, DOORA-BAREFIELD)   (CLARECASTLE, CAPT.)

Ollie Baker   *Colin Lynch 0-1*
(ST JOSEPH'S,   (ÉIRE ÓG)
DOORA-BAREFIELD)

Jamesie O'Connor 0-5   Fergus Tuohy 0-1   P. J. O'Connell 0-2
(ST JOSEPH'S,   (CLARECASTLE)   (CLARECASTLE)
DOORA-BAREFIELD)

Barry Murphy 0-1   Ger O'Loughlin 0-3   Stephen McNamara 0-1
(SCARRIFF)   (CLARECASTLE)   (ÉIRE ÓG)

Subs: David Forde (OGONOLLOE) *1-1 for McNamara, Andrew Whelan* (ST JOSEPH'S, DOORA-BAREFIELD) *for Murphy, Conor Clancy* (KILMALEY) *for Whelan. Also Brendan McNamara* (SCARRIFF), *Brian Quinn* (TULLA), *Fergus Hegarty* (KILNAMONA), *Eamonn Taaffe* (TUBBER), *Christy Chaplin* (SIXMILEBRIDGE), *Niall Gilligan* (SIXMILEBRIDGE)

SELECTORS
Ger Loughnane (MANAGER), *Michael McNamara, Tony Considine*

TIPPERARY
Brendan Cummins
(BALLYBACON-GRANGE)

Paul Shelly   *Noel Sheehy*   *Michael Ryan*
(KILLENAULE)   (SILVERMINES)   (UPPERCHURCH-DROMBANE)

Raymie Ryan   *Colm Bonnar*   *Conor Gleeson*
(CASHEL KING   (CASHEL KING   (BOHERLAHAN-DUALLA,
   CORMAC'S)   CORMAC'S)   CAPT.)

John Leahy 0-3   Aidan Butler
(MULLINAHONE)   (CLONOULTY-ROSSMORE)

Kevin Tucker 0-3   Declan Ryan 0-4   Tommy Dunne 0-7
(ÉIRE-ÓG, NENAGH) (CLONOULTY-ROSSMORE)   (TOOMEVARA)

Liam Cahill   Michael Cleary 0-1   Philip O'Dwyer
(BALLINGARRY)   (ÉIRE-ÓG, NENAGH)   (BOHERLAHAN-DUALLA)

Subs: Aidan Flanagan (BOHERLAHAN-DUALLA) for O'Dwyer, Conal
Bonnar (CASHEL KING CORMAC'S) for Gleeson. Also Kevin O'Sullivan
(CASHEL KING CORMAC'S), Liam Sheedy (PORTROE), Brendan Carroll
(THURLES SARSFIELDS), Brian O'Meara (MULLINAHONE), Brian
Gaynor (KILRUANE-MACDONAGHS), George Frend (TOOMEVARA),
Liam McGrath (BURGESS), Eugene O'Neill (CAPPAWHITE)

SELECTORS
Len Gaynor (MANAGER), Michael Doyle, Murt Duggan

REFEREE
Pat O'Connor
(LIMERICK)

18

2002: Waterford's return to glory

t may not have been as long as Clare's, but Waterford had endured a thirty-nine year famine before returning to glory with a Munster final victory over Tipperary at Páirc Uí Chaoimh on 30 June 2002. Their previous victory in 1963 over the same opposition was a much closer affair of three points. On this occasion the margin was eight points and should have been much greater, such was their second-half dominance when they outscored Tipperary by 1-13 to 2-2.

The Munster championship got off the ground with another Clare-Tipperary meeting at Páirc Uí Chaoimh on 19 May. It was the seventh meeting between the sides since 1997 and some of the excitement of the encounters had gone. This was reflected in the small attendance, less than 28,000, down one-third on the number that had attended some of the previous clashes.

Like many of these games, this was an intense affair with only two points between the sides at the final whistle. Tipperary went into the game as All-Ireland champions while Clare, under manager Cyril Lyons for the second year, were hoping for a reversal of the previous year's result. Clare had the better of the early exchanges and looked more threatening than Tipperary, but because of poor shooting found themselves a point behind, 0-4 to 0-3, after twenty minutes.

Then there was a dramatic development that had a major influence on the outcome of the game. Playing with a strong breeze a goal would have confirmed Clare's superiority, and it appeared certain when Niall Gilligan slipped his marker, Thomas Costello, and bore down on Cummins in the Tipperary goal. But, however he managed it, Cummins got to it, blocked the shot and sent a relieving clearance down the field.

Soon after, there was a similar happening at the other end. On this occasion Frank Lohan lost his footing, Eoin Kelly pounced on the ball, ran across the goal and rifled the ball past Davy Fitzgerald's ear. It was a body-blow to Clare. They did come back and got a goal before half-time, but Tipperary were ahead by 1-8 to 1-5 at the interval.

The game was notable for the failure of both centre backs. Seánie McMahon found Conor Gleeson more than his match, and David Kennedy couldn't manage Clare man-of-the-match, Tony Griffin, who played brilliantly and scored six points from play. Ultimately the difference between the sides was Eoin Kelly who scored 1-8.

After Tipperary scored their goal in the first half, the pattern of the game was set. Clare tried hard but never again regained parity. Every time they scored, Tipperary replied and always looked comfortable. The nearest Clare got was in the thirty-first minute of the second half when David Forde scored their second goal to bring them within a point, but Tipperary quickly responded with two points, and the final score was 1-18 to 2-13 in the champions' favour.

TIPPERARY
Brendan Cummins

Thomas Costello	Philip Maher	Donncha Fahey

Eamonn Corcoran	David Kennedy	Paul Kelly

Tommy Dunne (CAPT.) 0-2   Noel Morris 0-2

Brian O'Meara 0-1	Conor Gleeson 0-2	Lar Corbett

Eoin Kelly 1-8	John O'Brien 0-1	Eugene O'Neill 0-1

Subs: Mark O'Leary for Corbett, Benny Dunne 0-1 for O'Brien, Micheál Ryan for Mark O'Leary

Waterford had their first outing in a semi-final meeting with Cork at Semple Stadium a week later. For a team that hadn't won a Munster final for so long and one that had been at the receiving end of late defeats, this was to be a particularly sweet victory. It wasn't only a victory over Cork, but one that arrived in injury time when a Waterford clearance set up Ken McGrath for the match winner.

It was Waterford's fifth championship victory over Cork in twenty meetings over the previous forty years, and the man chiefly responsible for it was Paul Flynn, who accounted for twelve points of his side's total, nine of them from frees. It was Flynn's free-taking that kept Waterford in touch during the opening quarter when Cork were inclined to move ahead.

Waterford went ahead with a point after twenty-one minutes when John Mullane, who was causing Fergal Ryan problems, scored. About five minutes later, after Cusack saved brilliantly from Eoin McGrath, Cork were boosted by a goal from Eamonn Collins. The sides remained evenly matched during the rest of the half and Cork were just a point in front at the break, 1-7 to 0-9.

Waterford got a great boost in the forty-third minute when a long delivery from their midfielder, Tony Browne, bounced past Cusack into the Cork net. Two points in front and playing with more confidence, Waterford had extended their lead to five points within eight minutes of the restart. Cork were now under serious pressure and all they could manage in response was a point from a free by Ben O'Connor.

Waterford had been covering well in the back line, especially James Murray, who was very solid on Joe Deane. But Cork persistence paid off and in the course of a short period they shot three quick points to come within a score of Waterford. It took five more minutes for the equaliser to come from Deane.

In the remaining time Cork had two chances to go in front. Collins lost a chance and then Deane lost possession about fifty yards out after holding on too long to the ball. A draw looked inevitable until a Waterford clearance found Brian Greene and he set up Ken McGrath for the match winner forty seconds into injury time.

In the opinion of Cork team coach, Bertie Óg Murphy, the last five minutes were vital: 'After we had drawn level with five minutes to go, we were well on top but just couldn't go in front, and in such a tight situation it was always going to come down to who would win that one vital ball.'

It was a great result for Waterford and their new manager, Justin McCarthy: 'Overall, we turned in a great display and there is still a lot more left in the team.' He said he had always been a great admirer of Paul Flynn and that his point-scoring had been a big factor in their victory: 'His striking was immaculate and his shooting impeccable.'

There was controversy immediately after the game when Waterford defender Brian Flannery and man-of-the-match, Paul Flynn, refused to present themselves for drug testing after being randomly selected for the obligatory test by former international athlete, Al Guy. Their stance was fully backed by their team mates, but their actions made them liable to face a forty-eight week suspension under GAA rules. However, after about an hour's negotiations, they agreed to be tested and avoided suspension.

WATERFORD

Stephen Brenner

James Murray	*Tom Feeney*	*Brian Flannery*
Peter Queally	*Fergal Hartley* (CAPT.)	*Eoin Murphy*

Tony Browne 1-0   *Dave Bennett*

Eoin Kelly	*Andy Moloney*	*Paul Flynn 0-12*
John Mullane 0-1	*Séamus Prendergast 0-1*	*Eoin McGrath*

Subs: Ken McGrath 0-2 for Moloney, Dan Shanahan for Bennett, Micheál White for Mullane, Brian Greene for Eoin McGrath

Tipperary were as near perfection as possible in the second semi-final against Limerick at Cork on 2 June. The defence was outstanding with all six playing well, the midfield ruled the roost, and four of the forwards, five with the introduction of Benny Dunne, were performing well. The one Limerick man to stand out against this tide of success was Stephen McDonagh, who put up a stubborn defence at corner back.

Tipperary made a number of changes to the side that lined out against Clare. John Carroll came in at the edge of the square, while John O'Brien shifted out to the left wing, and Brian O'Meara moved across to mark Limerick captain, Mark Foley. The changes worked.

Limerick opened the scoring with a Mark Keane point before Tipperary replied with points from Kelly and Carroll. On a fine afternoon for hurling, scores were to prove hard to come by as defences were on top. The game appeared to change in the thirteenth minute when Ollie Moran struck a superb first-time shot to the corner of the Tipperary net to lift Limerick hopes.

For the next five minutes the game was in stalemate. After that Tipperary began to impose themselves. Conor Gleeson had a point and then Brian O'Meara, after a brilliant run, passed the ball to John Carroll, who blasted past Quaid in the Limerick goal.

More points followed, from Morris, Kelly and Carroll, to open up a five-point gap between the sides, 1-7 to 1-2. Between then and the break Tipperary had five more points to Limerick's four to leave the half-time score 1-12 to 1-6.

Although playing into the breeze in the second half, Tipperary had four points without reply to bring their lead to 1-16 to 1-6 with twenty minutes still to go. Limerick made changes. Four of their six forwards were replaced: Mike O'Brien by James Butler, Owen O'Neill by Barry Foley, Ollie Moran by Donie Ryan, Paul O'Grady by Clem Smith, and Limerick did outscore Tipperary during the period, but there was only going to be one winner, Tipperary, 1-20 to 1-13.

TIPPERARY

Brendan Cummins

Thomas Costello   *Philip Maher*   *Donncha Fahey*

Eamonn Corcoran   *David Kennedy*   *Paul Kelly*

Tommy Dunne (CAPT.) *0-1*   *Noel Morris 0-1*

Brian O'Meara 0-1 *Conor Gleeson 0-1*   *John O'Brien*

Eoin Kelly 0-12   *John Carroll 1-2*   *Eugene O'Neill*

Subs: Benny Dunne 0-2 for O'Neill, Paddy O'Brien for John O'Brien, Liam Cahill for Gleeson

Tipperary were immediately installed as favourites and no amount of warning from their management could prevent the players from becoming complacent about their chances as they listened to followers telling them they were 'sure things' and read newspaper eulogies about their achievements and potential. Manager Nicky English was at pains to paint Waterford in glowing colours, but it didn't dampen in any way the confidence of the Tipperary supporters, and like a pestilence it seeped into the minds of the players and diminished their performance on the day.

There was the other aspect of that victory over Limerick that few took into account. Limerick had performed dismally and the first to admit it was their manager, Eamon Cregan: 'Only about seven of our players were up to the required standard out there today. We should have been well up for the game, but to me it looked as if we lacked motivation and I must take responsibility for that. I won't blame the players. The buck stops with the manager. The way we played we don't deserve a second chance.'

The final was played at Páirc Uí Chaoimh on 30 June

before an attendance of close to 41,000, which included President Mary McAleese. After a stubborn first-half challenge, Tipperary were brushed aside with surprising ease by a remarkable display of power hurling by Waterford, which spoke volumes for the thoroughness of the preparation under their manager, Justin McCarthy. Motivated by a fanatical belief and performing with admirable style, Waterford had the cup won long before the final whistle sounded. It was a dramatic way to win a decider that had proved elusive for so long.

Waterford made a number of personnel and positional switches to the team that played in the semi-final. Brian Flannery switched to right corner back, while the pacey Brian Greene came in on the left to police Eoin Kelly. The half-back line remained the same with Peter Queally and Eoin Murphy changing wings. James Murray moved out from corner back to partner Tony Browne at centre field. Ken McGrath replaced Andy Moloney in the forwards and went full forward, with Séamus Prendergast moving out to the wing and Paul Flynn going to centre forward.

Tipperary made two changes in the forward line, Benny Dunne and Lar Corbett replacing John O'Brien and Eugene O'Neill.

Waterford showed great belief in their ability when, having won the toss, they opted to play against the breeze. Although Tipperary played well and got some good scores, with John Carroll and Eoin Kelly particularly threatening, Waterford held their own and edged in front in the sixteenth minute when Paul Flynn goaled from a twenty metre free. Many Waterford players were making an impact around the field, notably Ken McGrath, John Mullane and Séamus Prendergast in the forwards, while Fergal Hartley was dominant at centre back. Peter Queally was also effective in cutting off the supply of ball to Tipperary's inside forward line.

Tipperary regained the lead in the twenty-fifth minute with a point from Conor Gleeson just after they had a goal by Eoin Kelly disallowed because the umpire deemed that the ball was wide before Corbett passed it. However, it was Waterford who had the edge and this was reflected in their two-point lead by the thirty-second minute. At this stage Kelly put Tipperary back into the lead with a powerfully hit twenty metre free to give them the slenderest of advantages, 1-10 to 1-9, at the half-time whistle.

The story of the second half is easily told. For the first sixteen minutes the game remained close with the sides level on four occasions. Tipperary scored four times during that period, including two goals by Benny Dunne, and the score stood at 1-18 to 3-12 with fourteen minutes to go.

However, in the space of two minutes Waterford turned the tide irreversibly in their favour. Tony Browne whipped in a goal catching the defence off guard, after goalie Stephen Brenner sent a long free downfield, and beat the advancing Cummins.

The goal ignited the Decies men. Forgotten now were the many failures in the past, the numerous false dawns, as they realised that this was their greatest chance. Scenting victory, they took over with great assurance and dominated the game from end to end. Huge performances were the order of the day, especially from man-of-the-match, Ken McGrath, who got seven points from play, and from Fergal Hartley, Eoin Kelly, Eoin McGrath and John Mullane.

During this final period they scored 1-5 without reply from Tipperary, who failed to raise a flag in twenty minutes. It best reflected Waterford's complete takeover of the game and Tipperary's floundering in their wake. The final score was 2-23 to 3-12. The winners had 1-18 (nineteen scores) from play, as against 2-8 (ten scores) from the losers.

In the aftermath Nicky English admitted Tipperary were lucky to get away with an eight-point defeat: 'There isn't a team who would have lived with Waterford on that form,' he said. 'Once they settled they hurled superbly and had us in trouble in a lot of areas.'

For Waterford captain, Fergal Hartley, there was no better day: 'Days like this don't come too often for Waterford hurling,' he said. 'I just felt it in my bones that we would do the business today. Ours, at long last, is a team that believes in its own ability, and that self-belief which Justin has drilled into us carried us to new and spectacular heights today. It's a brilliant, brilliant feeling.'

WATERFORD

Stephen Brenner
(DE LA SALLE)

Brian Flannery	*Tom Feeney*	*Brian Greene*
(MOUNT SION)	(BALLYDUFF)	(MOUNT SION)

Eoin Murphy	*Fergal Hartley*	*Peter Queally*
(SHAMROCKS)	(BALLYGUNNER, CAPT.)	(BALLYDUFF)

Tony Browne 1-0   *James Murray*
(MOUNT SION)   (TALLOW)

Eoin Kelly 0-3	*Paul Flynn 1-6*	*Séamus Prendergast 0-1*
(MOUNT SION)	(BALLYGUNNER)	(ARDMORE)

John Mullane 0-4	*Ken McGrath 0-7*	*Eoin McGrath 0-1*
(DE LA SALLE)	(MOUNT SION)	(MOUNT SION)

Subs: Dave Bennett (LISMORE) 0-1 for Flannery, Micheál White (MOUNT SION) for Flynn, Andy Moloney (BALLYGUNNER) for Prendergast, Dan Shanahan (LISMORE) for Eoin McGrath. Also Noel Kelly (PORTLAW), James O'Connor (LISMORE), Declan Prendergast (ARDMORE), Pat Fitzgerald (CLARA), Conan Watt (DUNHILL), Brian Phelan (DE LA SALLE)

SELECTORS

Justin McCarthy, Colm Bonnar, Seamie Hannon

TIPPERARY

Brendan Cummins
(BALLYBACON-GRANGE)

Thomas Costello	*Philip Maher*	*Donncha Fahey*

(CAPPAWHITE)   (BORRISOLEIGH)   (ST MARY'S)

Eamonn Corcoran   David Kennedy   Paul Kelly
(J. K. BRACKENS) (LOUGHMORE-CASTLEINEY)   (MULLINAHONE)

Tommy Dunne 0-2   Noel Morris
(TOOMEVARA, CAPT.) (LOUGHMORE-CASTLEINEY)

Benny Dunne 2-2   Conor Gleeson 0-2   Brian O'Meara
(TOOMEVARA)   (BOHERLAHAN-DUALLA)   (MULLINAHONE)

Eoin Kelly 1-4   John Carroll 0-1   Lar Corbett 0-1
(MULLINAHONE)   (ROSCREA)   (THURLES SARSFIELDS)

Subs: Eddie Enright (THURLES SARSFIELDS) for Morris, Paul Ormonde (LOUGHMORE-CASTLEINEY) for Kennedy, Mark O'Leary (KILRUANE-MACDONAGHS) for Costello, Paddy O'Brien (TOOMEVARA) for Gleeson. Also Justin Cottrell (TOOMEVARA), Séamus Butler (DROM INCH), Liam Cahill (BALLINGARRY), Paul Curran (MULLINAHONE), John Devane (CLONOULTY-ROSSMORE), Ken Dunne (TOOMEVARA), Brian Horgan ((KICKHAMS), Colin Morrissey (GALTEE ROVERS), Eugene O'Neill (CAPPAWHITE), Micheál Ryan (TEMPLEDERRY)

SELECTORS
Nicky English (MANAGER), Jack Bergin, Ken Hogan

REFEREE
Aodán Mac Suibhne
(DUBLIN)

19

2004: *Waterford triumph again*

Waterford had hoped to make it back-to-back Munster finals in 2003, but it wasn't to be. They did look good in the final at half-time when they led by 1-9 to 1-4 after dominating the first half. In fact Cork's goal by Setanta Ó hAilpin was against the run of play. But Cork, with the aid of the breeze, were rampant in the second half and even a brilliant display by John Mullane — he scored 3-1 in the course of the hour — couldn't prevent Waterford from losing once again to their old rivals. This defeat must have been foremost in the minds of the players when the sides met once again in the 2004 final at Thurles.

The two first-round games in the championship were played on 16 May. Cork had Kerry at home in Páirc Uí

Chaoimh and there was no major surprise when they scored a facile victory by 4-19 to 1-7.

Waterford had an equally easy win over Clare at Semple Stadium on the same day. It was a big bounce back for the winners in the light of their loss to Galway in the National League final the previous Sunday. In fact they were anything but impressive when losing by five points. On this occasion they were brilliant, enjoying a runaway win over an inept Clare challenge.

There were nineteen points between the sides at the end, 3-21 to 1-8. Waterford led from start to finish, with Clare waiting twenty-seven minutes for their first score. Dan Shanahan finished with a hat-trick of goals in only his second championship start under Justin McCarthy. But Shanahan wasn't the only Waterford man to sparkle. There were also outstanding performances from midfielder Eoin Kelly, Ken McGrath and John Mullane.

By the time Colin Lynch got Clare's first score, Waterford had a tally of 1-6, the goal coming from Shanahan after a pass from Bennett. They remained in control until just before half-time when they conceded a penalty which was put away by Tony Griffin from a rebound. It left Clare trailing by six points at the interval, 2-7 to 1-4. They were to add only four further points during the second half, while Waterford were rampant, going on to win in a canter.

The result was a sensation. Clare were expected to be a force in the game and, in the aftermath of Waterford's poor performance in the league final, were slight favourites. Waterford's performance surprised everyone, even their most ardent supporters, and they caught Clare completely by surprise.

WATERFORD
Stephen Brenner

Eoin Murphy   *Tom Feeney*   *James Murray*

Tony Browne   *Ken McGrath* (CAPT.)   *Brian Phelan*

Dave Bennett 0-5   *Eoin Kelly 0-8*

Dan Shanahan 3-1   *Michael Walsh 0-1*   *Paul Flynn 0-1*

John Mullane 0-4   *Séamus Prendergast 0-1*   *Eoin McGrath*

Subs: Paul O'Brien for Paul Flynn, Seán Ryan for Eoin McGrath, Andy Moloney for Séamus Prendergast

There were three points between the sides at the end of the semi-final meeting between Cork and Limerick at the Gaelic Grounds on 30 May. Many saw the turning point in the game six minutes into the second half when a seventy-five metre free by Cork captain, Ben O'Connor, went all the way to the Limerick net through the fingers of the unvisored Limerick goalkeeper, Albert Shanahan. It was an unfortunate blow for Limerick, who were leading by a point at the time and holding their own.

Limerick had got off to a flying start with a goal after seven minutes from full forward Seán O'Connor. They showed excellent composure, scoring some fine long-range points. However, they missed scoring opportunities also and fell down on their free-taking. They should have been more ahead than 1-5 to 0-7 at the interval, especially as Cork were in partial disarray.

The Cork selectors made a number of changes at half-time, most of which worked. Switching John Gardiner to wing back and bringing Tom Kenny to centre field worked very effectively. The decision to bring on Brian Corcoran was also a good one. O'Connor's goal put them in the driving seat and they played brilliantly for about fifteen minutes to go seven points ahead by the sixty-seventh minute.

The game seemed to be heading for a predictable outcome until Seán O'Connor had his second goal to give Limerick renewed hope. Soon after, substitute Patrick Tobin pointed to reduce the margin to a goal and raise the possibility of a Limerick win. But there were no further scores and Cork went through to the Munster final 1-18 to 2-12.

In the post-mortems on the game there were question marks about Cork's performance. The team that lined out was by no means a settled unit. Much was learned in the course of the game and the fifteen that finished the hour were much more the settled side. Cork were heavily dependent on frees with 1-10 of their 1-18 coming from placed balls, Ben O'Connor contributing 1-8 of the total. There was also a question about their killer instinct and about the way they let Limerick back into the game during the last eight minutes.

The second semi-final between Waterford and Tipperary at Cork on 6 June was a rip-roaring contest. Waterford got off to a whirlwind start with two goals by Dan Shanahan, led by 3-5 to 2-5 at half-time, had to contend with an improved Tipperary performance in the second half, and depended on a goal by substitute Paul O'Brien a minute and a half before the end of normal time to gain victory by 4-10 to 3-12. On the other side there was some wonderful goalkeeping by Brendan Cummins, who got poor enough cover from a Tipperary back line, with the exception of Philip Maher.

Waterford achieved their victory without the services of one of their most celebrated names, Tony Browne, who failed a last-minute fitness test. They lost two other star players, Paul Flynn and Ken McGrath, through injury in the last ten minutes. On the other hand, they were extremely fortunate in the performances of substitutes Brian Wall and Paul O'Brien. Declan Prendergast was in at full back in place of Tom Feeney and Brian Wall substituted for Tony Browne.

Waterford started well, particularly in defence, with both Eoin Murphy and James Murray prominent. Once Eoin Kelly settled he posed the only real threat for Tipperary, but his attempt at a goal from a twenty metre free in the sixth minute was cleared. Scores were few and far between until the twentieth minute when Dan Shanahan goaled. He followed with a second four minutes later to put Waterford 2-3 to 0-2 in front.

However, within less than three minutes Tipperary's

Eoin Kelly's brilliance changed the picture dramatically. First he goaled from a Benny Dunne opening, then pointed, and again found the net with a shot that Stephen Brenner made a poor effort at stopping.

After that there was a period of dominance by both defences with few scores coming. In the last five minutes of the half, John Mullane broke through for a spectacular goal, and at half-time it was 3-5 to 2-5 in Waterford's favour.

Eoin Kelly, who had got all but one point of the Tipperary total in the first half, opened the second half with two pointed frees. Colin Morrissey had one in between. Another Kelly effort was waved inexplicably wide before he got another from almost the same position. After the latter score in the fifty-fifth minute, Kelly had only one further point in the remaining time.

Kelly's marker, James Murray, stuck gamely to his task of trying to control him and became more effective as the game wore on. There was the other factor that the supply of ball to Kelly's corner became scarcer. This was due to the increased influence of Ken McGrath and Brian Phelan in the half-back line and the growing dominance of Eoin Kelly at centre field. In the forward line Séamus Prendergast, who was providing the thrust for Waterford, hit two valuable points and made the opening for the goal near the end.

Cummins was performing heroics in the Tipperary goal, making spectacular double saves from O'Brien and Flynn in quick succession. The second led to a 70 which Bennett put over to put Waterford two points clear. Scores became fewer and wides began to mount as the game reached its climax. It looked as if the game would go Tipperary's way after Morrissey goaled to give them a two-point advantage.

Ken McGrath and Mullane wasted chances for Waterford before O'Brien seized an opportunity and had the ball in the net for a one-point lead. As the game continued, Tipperary had three chances of varying possibilities, but stalwart defending by the Waterford backs kept their goal intact and they clung on for a 4-10 to 3-12 victory.

Manager Justin McCarthy was jubilant, believing that the victory would bring the team on even further as they prepared for a repeat of the previous year's decider against Cork. He spoke of the great belief among the players who were maturing all the time. 'There is great leadership, and that rates very highly with me,' he said.

WATERFORD

Stephen Brenner

Eoin Murphy   *Declan Prendergast*   *James Murray*

Brian Phelan   *Ken McGrath* (CAPT.)   *Brian Wall*

Dave Bennett 0-2   *Eoin Kelly 0-2*

Dan Shanahan 2-0   *Michael Walsh 0-1*   *Paul Flynn 0-2*

John Mullane 1-0   *Séamus Prendergast 0-2*   *Eoin McGrath 0-1*

Subs: Paul O'Brien 1-0 for Eoin McGrath, Shane O'Sullivan for Paul Flynn, Tom Feeney for Ken McGrath

Waterford were contesting their third Munster final in a row when they lined out against Cork at Thurles on 27 June. Only once before had this happened, in 1957, 58 and 59, when they went on to capture the All-Ireland title for only the second, and last, time in their history. Cork went into the final slight favourites, based more on tradition and experience than the relative merits of the teams. Waterford, because of their tendency to play beneath themselves in vital matches, were regarded as an uncertain quantity. As it turned out, it was Waterford who showed more character and belief especially in the second half, and this brought them to their first victory in a final over Cork in forty-five years.

Cork had a whirlwind start, hit the ground running and had a goal very early on when a ground shot from newcomer Garvan McCarthy slipped through Stephen Brenner's legs.

In another four minutes they were leading by 1-3 to 0-1 after John Gardiner had made the first of two key interceptions which denied Dan Shanahan goal opportunities. Seán Óg Ó hAilpín was to the fore at right half-back and Jerry O'Connor was very sharp at centre field. The forwards were getting plenty of ball and creating many problems for the Waterford backs as they ran at them. Ben O'Connor and Joe Deane were particularly effective.

On the Waterford side John Mullane and Paul Flynn were finding it hard to make a mark. In contrast, Dan Shanahan was on top of his game and scored three of the opening four points. It took a goal by Eoin Kelly, following a great solo run in the fifteenth minute, to rally Waterford's flagging spirits.

A great Brian Corcoran point from near the sideline put Cork five points in front by the twenty-fifth minute, but almost immediately Dan Shanahan lifted Waterford with a stunning goal after catching a high ball over Diarmuid O'Sullivan's head at the edge of the Cork square. Two further points from Ken McGrath and Flynn put Waterford back in the hunt and they were only three points in arrears, 1-14 to 2-8, at the break.

Cork moved Ó hAilpín on to Shanahan in the second half and it was an important move in curbing him. He hit two wides in the early minutes but was relatively quiet after that.

More significant than the curbing of Shanahan was the sending off of John Mullane soon after the resumption for an off-the-ball incident with Brian Murphy. Many believed this marked the end of Waterford's chances. Instead, Waterford responded magnificently to their adversity. They produced some superb individual displays, especially from Paul Flynn and Ken McGrath, but also an overall team effort. As well as being short a player, Waterford were also playing into the breeze in the second half.

As it happened the wind proved a disadvantage to Cork. Playing the extra man behind the half-back line, they managed a lot of long clearances, but the quality of ball delivered to their inside forwards was poor. As well, Waterford had rearranged their inside back line and greatly reduced the danger of their opposites. Also, the finishing of the Cork forwards was poor, with the result that Waterford were only two points in arrears by the fiftieth minute. At this stage a goal by Flynn put them in front, but Deane levelled for Cork within two minutes. Ben O'Connor and Eoin Kelly swapped points.

After this, and in spite of being short a man, Waterford made all the running. Ken McGrath and Tony Browne were inspiring. Declan Prendergast, Eoin Kelly and Michael Walsh played their hearts out, and up front Paul Flynn completed a great team effort with vital scores.

The game could have gone either way. Cork had bad luck when a pass from substitute Jonathan O'Callaghan looked certain to set up Ben O'Connor for a goal in the sixty-eighth minute, except that it was deflected into the hand of Declan Prendergast and cleared.

The game could even have ended in a draw after a Tom Kenny score in the second-last minute left Waterford hanging on by one point. A high ball was dropped around the Waterford half-back line to be contested by Diarmuid O'Sullivan, who had moved upfield, and Waterford captain Ken McGrath. McGrath plucked the ball out of the air and won a free. It was the defining moment. The game was over and Waterford had won by 3-16 to 1-21.

The refusal to roll over and die when adversity struck at the beginning of the second half revealed Waterford's great character. They had a huge task in hand and they rose to the challenge magnificently. As well as the team performing brilliantly, the sideline people also excelled themselves, switching the players around to counteract any danger and achieve better performances. Those of Ken McGrath and Paul Flynn in the last quarter were out of the top drawer. Another factor in Waterford's triumph was the skill of so many of their players at catching the high ball to win primary possession.

WATERFORD

Stephen Brenner
(DE LA SALLE)

James Murray	*Declan Prendergast*	*Eoin Murphy*
(TALLOW)	(ARDMORE)	(SHAMROCKS)

Tony Browne	*Ken McGrath 0-1*	*Brian Phelan*
(MOUNT SION)	(MOUNT SION, CAPT.)	(DE LA SALLE)

Dave Bennett 0-1   *Eoin Kelly 1-1*
(LISMORE)   (MOUNT SION)

Dan Shanahan 1-3	*Michael Walsh*	*Paul Flynn 1-7*
(LISMORE)	(STRADBALLY)	(BALLYGUNNER)

John Mullane 0-2	*Séamus Prendergast 0-1*	*Eoin McGrath*
(DE LA SALLE)	(ARDMORE)	(MOUNT SION)

*Subs: Paul O'Brien (*TALLOW*) for Dave Bennett, Shane O'Sullivan (*BALLYGUNNER*) for Eoin McGrath, Jack Kennedy (*BALLYDUFF LOWER*) for Paul O'Brien. Also Ian O'Regan (*MOUNT SION*), Tom Feeney (*SARSFIELDS*), Brian Wall (*FOURMILEWATER*), Andy Moloney (*BALLYGUNNER*), Liam Lawlor (*FOURMILEWATER*), David O'Brien (*TALLOW*), Seán Ryan (*MOUNT SION*), Ger Quinlan (*ROANMORE*), Denis Coffey (*ST MARY'S*), John Wall (*COLLIGAN ROCKIES*), Andrew Kirwan (*PORTLAW*), Wayne Hutchinson (*BALLYGUNNER*)*

SELECTORS

*Justin McCarthy (*MANAGER*), Seamie Hannon, Nicky Cashin, Kevin Ryan*

CORK

Donal Óg Cusack
(CLOYNE)

Wayne Sherlock	*Diarmuid O'Sullivan*	*Brian Murphy*
(BLACKROCK)	(CLOYNE)	(BRIDE ROVERS)

Seán Óg Ó hAilpin *Ronan Curran 0-1*   *John Gardiner*
(NA PIARSAIGH)   (ST FINBARR'S)   (NA PIARSAIGH)

Tom Kenny 0-3   *Jerry O'Connor 0-2*
(GRENAGH)   (NEWTOWNSHANDRUM)

Garvan McCarthy 1-0 *Niall McCarthy*   *Timmy McCarthy*
(SARSFIELDS)   (CARRIGTWOHILL)   (CASTLELYONS)

Ben O'Connor 0-4   *Brian Corcoran 0-2*   *Joe Deane 0-9*
(NEWTOWNSHANDRUM, CAPT.)(ERIN'S OWN)   (KILLEAGH)

Subs: Jonathan O'Callaghan (CASTLETOWNROCHE) *for Niall McCarthy, Kieran Murphy* (SARSFIELDS) *for Garvan McCarthy, Cian O'Connor* (ERIN'S OWN) *for John Gardiner. Also Paul Morrissey* (NEWTOWNSHANDRUM), *John Browne* (BLACKROCK), *Graham Callinan* (GLEN ROVERS), *Michael O'Connell* (MIDLETON), *Paul Tierney* (BLACKROCK), *John Anderson* (GLEN ROVERS), *Martin Coleman* (BALLINHASSIG), *Eamonn Collins* (VALLEY ROVERS), *Michael Byrne* (KILLEAGH)

SELECTORS

Donal O'Grady (COACH), *Pat Morrissey, Seánie O'Leary, Fred Sheedy, John Allen*

REFEREE

Seánie McMahon
(CLARE)

Index

(Note: entries preceded by the letter p refer to the picture number)